Level 1

BENCHMARK SERIES

Microsoft®

Excel

365

2019 Edition

Review and Assessment

Nita Rutkosky | **Audrey Roggenkamp**
Pierce College Puyallup
Puyallup, Washington

| **Ian Rutkosky**
Pierce College Puyallup
Puyallup, Washington

PARADIGM
EDUCATION SOLUTIONS

Minneapolis

Vice President, Content and Digital Solutions: Christine Hurney
Director of Content Development: Carley Fruzetti
Developmental Editor: Jennifer Joline Anderson
Director of Production: Timothy W. Larson
Production Editor/Project Manager: Jen Weaverling
Senior Design and Production Specialist: Jack Ross
Cover and Interior Design: Valerie King
Copy Editor: Communicáto, Ltd.
Testers: Janet Blum, Traci Post
Indexer: Terry Casey
Vice President, Director of Digital Products: Chuck Bratton
Digital Projects Manager: Tom Modl
Digital Solutions Manager: Gerry Yumul
Senior Director of Digital Products and Onboarding: Christopher Johnson
Supervisor of Digital Products and Onboarding: Ryan Isdahl
Vice President, Marketing: Lara Weber McLellan
Marketing and Communications Manager: Selena Hicks

Care has been taken to verify the accuracy of information presented in this book. However, the authors, editors, and publisher cannot accept responsibility for web, email, newsgroup, or chat room subject matter or content, or for consequences from the application of the information in this book, and make no warranty, expressed or implied, with respect to its content.

Trademarks: Microsoft is a trademark or registered trademark of Microsoft Corporation in the United States and/or other countries. Some of the product names and company names included in this book have been used for identification purposes only and may be trademarks or registered trade names of their respective manufacturers and sellers. The authors, editors, and publisher disclaim any affiliation, association, or connection with, or sponsorship or endorsement by, such owners.

Paradigm Education Solutions is independent from Microsoft Corporation and not affiliated with Microsoft in any manner.

Cover Photo Credit: © lowball-jack/GettyImages

We have made every effort to trace the ownership of all copyrighted material and to secure permission from copyright holders. In the event of any question arising as to the use of any material, we will be pleased to make the necessary corrections in future printings.

ISBN 978-0-76388-725-4 (print)

Contents

Microsoft® Excel® Level 1

Unit 1

Preparing and Formatting Worksheets

CHAPTER

1

Preparing an Excel Workbook

 The online course includes additional review and assessment resources.

Skills Assessment

Create a Worksheet Using AutoCorrect and AutoComplete

1. Create the worksheet shown in Figure 1.1 with the following specifications:
   a. To create the copyright symbol (©) in cell A1, type (c).
   b. Type the misspelled words as shown and let the AutoCorrect feature correct them. Use the AutoComplete feature to insert the second occurrences of *Category, Available,* and *Balance.*
   c. Merge and center cells A1 and B1.
2. Save the workbook and name it **1-Plan**.
3. Print and then close **1-Plan**.

Figure 1.1 Assessment 1

	A	B	C
1	Premier Plan©		
2	Plan A	Catagory	
3		Available	
4		Balence	
5	Plan B	Category	
6		Available	
7		Balance	
8			

Create and Format a Worksheet

1. Create the worksheet shown in Figure 1.2 with the following specifications:
   a. Merge and center the range A1:C1 and then type the data in the cells as shown in Figure 1.2.
   b. After typing the data, automatically adjust the width of column A.
   c. Insert a SUM function in cell B8 that sums the amounts in the range B3:B7 and insert a SUM function in cell C8 that sums the amounts in the range C3:C7.
   d. Apply the Accounting format with no digits after the decimal point to the ranges B3:C3 and B8:C8.

e. Apply the Comma format with no digits after the decimal point to the range B4:C7.
f. If any number amount displays as number symbols (###), automatically adjust the width of the appropriate column.
2. Save the workbook and name it **1-Exp**.
3. Print and then close **1-Exp**.

Figure 1.2 Assessment 2

	A	B	C
1	Construction Project		
2	Expense	Original	Current
3	Material	129000	153000
4	Labor	97000	98500
5	Equipment rental	14500	11750
6	Permits	1200	1350
7	Tax	1950	2145
8	Total		
9			

Assessment 3

Create a Worksheet Using the Fill Handle

1. Type the worksheet data shown in Figure 1.3 with the following specifications:
   a. Type Monday in cell B2 and then use the fill handle to fill in the remaining days of the week.
   b. Type 350 in cell B3 and then use the fill handle to fill in the remaining numbers in the row.
   c. Merge and center the range A1:G1.
2. Insert a SUM function in cell G3 that sums the amounts in the range B3:F3 and insert a SUM function in cell G4 that sums the amounts in the range B4:F4.
3. After typing the data, select the range B3:G4 and then apply the Accounting format with two digits shown past the decimal point.
4. If necessary, adjust the column widths.
5. Save the workbook and name it **1-Invest**.
6. Print and then close **1-Invest**.

Figure 1.3 Assessment 3

	A	B	C	D	E	F	G
1		CAPITAL INVESTMENTS					
2		Monday	Tuesday	Wednesday	Thursday	Friday	Total
3	Budget	350	350	350	350	350	
4	Actual	310	425	290	375	400	
5							

Insert Formulas in a Worksheet

1. Open **DIAnalysis** and then save it with the name **1-DIAnalysis**.
2. Insert a SUM function in cell B15 that sums the amounts in the range B4:B14.
3. Use the fill handle to copy the formula in cell B15 to cell C15.
4. Insert a formula in cell D4 that averages the amounts in cells B4 and C4.
5. Use the fill handle to copy the formula in cell D4 to the range D5:D15 and fill without formatting. *Hint: Click the Auto Fill Options button that appears after filling the range to display additional auto fill options.*
6. Save, print, and then close **1-DIAnalysis**.

Visual Benchmark

Create, Format, and Insert Formulas in a Worksheet

1. At a blank workbook, create the worksheet shown in Figure 1.4 with the following specifications:
   a. Type data in the cells as shown in the figure. Use the fill handle when appropriate, merge and center the text *Personal Expenses - July through December*, and automatically adjust the column widths.
   b. Insert formulas to determine averages and totals.
   c. Apply the Accounting format with no digits after the decimal point to the amounts in the range B3:H3 and the range B11:H11.
   d. Apply the Comma format with no digits after the decimal point to the amounts in the range B4:H10.
2. Save the workbook and name it **1-PersExps**.
3. Print and then close **1-PersExps**.

Figure 1.4 Visual Benchmark

	A	B	C	D	E	F	G	H
1				Personal Expenses - July through December				
2	Expense	July	August	September	October	November	December	Average
3	Rent	850	850	850	850	850	850	
4	Rental insurance	55	55	55	55	55	55	
5	Health insurance	120	120	120	120	120	120	
6	Electricity	129	135	126	150	225	240	
7	Utilities	53	62	49	32	55	61	
8	Telephone	73	73	73	73	73	73	
9	Groceries	143	137	126	150	147	173	
10	Gasoline	89	101	86	99	76	116	
11	Total							
12								

Case Study

Part 1

You are the office manager for Deering Industries. One of your responsibilities is to create a monthly calendar containing information on staff meetings, training, and due dates for time cards. Open **DICalendar** and then insert the following information:

- Type November 2021 in cell A2.
- Insert the days of the week (*Sunday*, *Monday*, *Tuesday*, *Wednesday*, *Thursday*, *Friday*, and *Saturday*) in the range A3:G3. (Use the fill handle to fill in the days of the week and fill without formatting.)
- Insert the numbers *1* through *6* in the range B4:G4.
- Insert in the calendar the remaining numbers of the days (numbers *7* through *13* in the range A6:G6, numbers *14* through *20* in the range A8:G8, numbers *21* through *27* in the range A10:G10, and numbers *28* through *30* in the range A12:C12. If you use the fill handle, fill without formatting.)
- Excel training will be held Thursday, November 4, from 9:00 to 11:00 a.m. Insert this information in cell E5. (Insert the text on two lines by typing Excel Training, pressing Alt + Enter to move the insertion point to the next line, and then typing 9-11 a.m.)
- A staff meeting is held the second and fourth Monday of each month from 9:00 to 11:00 a.m. Insert this information in cell B7 and cell B11.
- Time cards are due the first and third Fridays of the month. Insert information indicating that time cards are due in cells F5 and F9.
- A production team meeting is scheduled for Tuesday, November 23, from 1:00 to 3:00 p.m. Insert this information in cell C11.

Save the workbook and name it **1-DICalendar**. Print and then close the workbook.

Part 2

The purchasing department manager at Deering Industries has asked you to prepare a worksheet containing information on quarterly purchases. Open **DIExpenditures** and then insert data as shown in Figure 1.5. After typing the data, insert formulas in the appropriate cells to calculate averages and totals. Apply the Comma format to the range F5:F8. Save the workbook and name it **1-DIExpenditures**. Print and then close the workbook.

Figure 1.5 Visual Benchmark

	A	B	C	D	E	F
1						
2		PURCHASING DEPARTMENT - EXPENDITURES				
3	*Category*					*Average*
4	Supplies	$ 645.75	$ 756.25	$ 534.78	$ 789.50	
5	Equipment	4,520.55	10,789.35	3,825.00	12,890.72	
6	Furniture	458.94	2,490.72	851.75	743.20	
7	Training	1,000.00	250.00	1,200.00	800.00	
8	Software	249.00	1,574.30	155.45	3,468.70	

Part 3

The manager of the Deering Industries Purchasing Department has asked you to prepare a note to the finances coordinator, Ms. Strauss. In Word, type a note to Jennifer Strauss explaining that you have prepared an Excel worksheet with the Purchasing Department expenditures. You are including the cells from the worksheet containing the expenditure information. In Excel, open **1-DIExpenditures**, copy the range A3:F9, and then paste the cells in the Word document. Make any corrections to the table so the information is readable. Save the document and name it **1-DINotetoJS**. Print and then close the document. Close **1-DIExpenditures**.

Part 4

You will be ordering copy machines for several departments in Deering Industries and have decided to research prices. Using the internet, find three companies that sell copiers and record information on different copier models. Open **DICopiers** and then type the company names, model numbers, and prices in the designated cells. Save the completed workbook and name it **1-DICopiers**. Print and then close **1-DICopiers**.

Inserting Formulas in a Worksheet

 The online course includes additional review and assessment resources.

Skills Assessment

Assessment

1

Insert AVERAGE, MAX, and MIN Functions

1. Open **DISales** and then save it with the name **2-DISales**.
2. Use the AVERAGE function to determine the monthly sales (the range H4:H9).
3. Apply the Accounting format with no digits after the decimal point to cell H4.
4. Total each monthly column, including the *Average* column (the range B10:H10).
5. In cell B11, use the MAX function to determine the highest monthly total (for the range B10:G10).
6. In cell B12, use the MIN function to determine the lowest monthly total (for the range B10:G10).
7. Save, print, and then close **2-DISales**.

Assessment

2

Insert the SUM Function and Enter Formulas with Mathematical Operators

1. Open **CMIncome** and then save it with the name **2-CMIncome**.
2. The manager of Capstan Marine needs a condensed quarterly statement of income for the third quarter. Insert each of the following formulas by typing it, by using the pointing method, or by using the AutoSum button:
   a. In cell B7, subtract cost of goods sold from sales by entering =b5-b6.
   b. In cell B12, add the three expenses by entering =sum(b9:b11).
   c. In cell B14, subtract total expenses from gross margin by entering =b7-b12.
   d. In cell B15, multiply net income before taxes by 22% and then subtract that value from net income before taxes by entering =b14-(b14*22%).
3. Relatively copy the formulas in column B to columns C and D using the fill handle as follows:
   a. Copy the formula in cell B7 to the range C7:D7.
   b. Copy the formula in cell B12 to the range C12:D12.
   c. Copy the formula in cell B14 to the range C14:D14.
   d. Copy the formula in cell B15 to the range C15:D15.
4. Insert the total in cell E5 by using the AutoSum button to add the values in the range B5:D5.
5. Use the fill handle to copy the SUM function in cell E5 to the range E6:E15. (Cells E8 and E13 will contain hyphens.)
6. Delete the contents of cells E8 and E13.

7. Apply the Accounting format with a dollar symbol and one digit displayed past the decimal point to the range B5:E5.
8. Insert a TODAY function in cell A18.
9. Save, print, and then close **2-CMIncome**.

Write Formulas with Absolute Cell References

1. Open **CCQuotas** and then save it with the name **2-CCQuotas**.
2. Make the following changes to the worksheet:
   a. Insert a formula using an absolute reference to determine the projected quotas with a 10% increase from the current quota (multiply the current quota by the increase in cell B15).
   b. Copy the formula in cell C4 to the range C5:C13.
   c. Save and then print **2-CCQuotas**.
   d. Determine the projected quotas with a 15% increase from the current quota by changing cell A15 to *15% Increase* and cell B15 to *1.15*.
   e. Save and then print **2-CCQuotas**.
   f. Determine the projected quotas with a 20% increase from the current quota.
3. Apply the Accounting format with no digits after the decimal point to cell C4.
4. Save, print, and then close **2-CCQuotas**.

Write Formulas with Mixed Cell References

1. Open **AASMileage** and then save it with the name **2-AASMileage**.
2. Determine the mileage range of vehicles with different miles per gallon and fuel tank capacities by following these steps:
   a. In cell C5, multiply the vehicle fuel tank capacity by the vehicle miles per gallon rating by entering $=b5*c4$.
   b. Change the cell references in the formula so when it is copied, it will multiply the correct values in the chart. Either type dollar symbols in the formula or press the F4 function key until the correct mixed cell references display. *Hint: Refer to Activity 3d for assistance.*
   c. Use the fill handle to complete the chart (fill without formatting).
3. Save, print, and then close **2-AASMileage**.

Use Help to Learn about Excel Options

1. Learn more about using parentheses within formulas by completing the following steps:
   a. At a blank workbook, display the Help task pane and then search for information on the order in which Excel performs operations in formulas.
   b. Read the information about using parentheses in formulas.
   c. Close the Help task pane.
2. Open **ParenFormulas** and then save it with the name **2-ParenFormulas**.
3. Change the results of the formulas individually (do not use the fill handle) in the range B6:B10 by editing the formulas to include parentheses. Consider writing the formulas on paper before inserting them in the cells. *Note: The formulas may require multiple sets of parentheses.*
4. Once the formulas have been edited, compare the new results with the values in column C.
5. Make sure that *YES* displays in column D for each formula.
6. Turn on the display of formulas.
7. Save, print, and then close **2-ParenFormulas**.

Visual Benchmark

Create a Worksheet and Insert Formulas

1. At a blank workbook, type the data in the cells indicated in Figure 1.1 but **do not** type the data in the following cells. Instead, insert the formulas as indicated:

   - In the range D3:D9, insert a formula that calculates the salaries.
   - In the range D14:D19, insert a formula that calculates the differences.
   - In the range B29:D29, insert a formula that calculates the averages.
   - In the range E24:E28, insert a formula that calculates the weighted average of test scores. *Hint: Refer to Activity 3b, Step 2, for assistance on writing a formula that determines weighted averages.*

   The results of your formulas should match the results shown in in the figure.

2. Apply any other formatting needed so your worksheet looks similar to the worksheet shown in Figure 1.1.
3. Save the workbook and name it **2-Formulas**.
4. Print **2-Formulas**.
5. Turn on the display of formulas and then print the worksheet again.
6. Turn off the display of formulas and then close the workbook.

Figure 1.1 Visual Benchmark

	A	B	C	D	E
1		Weekly Payroll			
2	Employee	Hours	Rate	Salary	
3	Alvarez, Rita	40	$ 22.50	$ 900.00	
4	Campbell, Owen	15	22.50	337.50	
5	Heitmann, Luanne	25	19.00	475.00	
6	Malina, Susan	40	18.75	750.00	
7	Parker, Kenneth	40	18.75	750.00	
8	Reitz, Collette	20	15.00	300.00	
9	Shepard, Gregory	15	12.00	180.00	
10					
11					
12		Construction Projects			
13	Project	Projected	Actual	Difference	
14	South Cascade	$145,000	$ 141,597	$ (3,403)	
15	Rogue River Park	120,000	124,670	4,670	
16	Meridian	120,500	99,450	(21,050)	
17	Lowell Ridge	95,250	98,455	3,205	
18	Walker Canyon	70,000	68,420	(1,580)	
19	Nettleson Creek	52,000	49,517	(2,483)	
20					
21					
22		Test Scores			
23	Employee	Test No. 1	Test No. 2	Test No. 3	Wgt. Avg.
24	Coffey, Annette	62%	64%	76%	70%
25	Halverson, Ted	88%	96%	90%	91%
26	Kohler, Jeremy	80%	76%	82%	80%
27	McKnight, Carol	68%	72%	78%	74%
28	Parkhurst, Jody	98%	96%	98%	98%
29	Test Averages	79%	81%	85%	
30	Test Weights	25%	25%	50%	

Case Study

Part 1

You are the office manager for Allenmore Auto Sales and are responsible for preparing the monthly sales worksheet. Open **AASFebSales** and then save it with the name **2-AASFebSales**. Complete the workbook by inserting the following formulas:

- In column F, insert a formula that calculates the gross profit, which is the price minus the dealer cost.
- In column H, insert a formula that multiplies the gross profit by the commission percentage.
- In column I, insert a formula that calculates the net profit, which is the gross profit minus the total commission.
- Apply the Accounting format to the amounts in cells D4, E4, F4, H4, and I4.

Save the workbook, print the workbook (it will print on two pages), and then close the workbook.

Part 2

The sales manager at Allenmore Auto Sales has asked you to determine the percentage of the total commission that each salesperson has earned for February. Open **AASFebCom** and then save it with the name **2-AASFebCom**. Insert a formula in cell C5 that divides cell B5 by the amount in cell C3. Use an absolute cell reference for cell C3 when writing the formula. Copy the formula to the range C6:C12. Save, print, and then close the workbook.

Part 3

In your position at Allenmore Auto Sales, you have created a workbook for automobile trade-ins for February. The sales manager wants used automobiles to be wholesaled if they are not sold within a specific period of time. She wants you to determine the date each February trade-in is to be wholesaled. She wants any used automobile older than 2013 to be wholesaled after 45 days and any automobile newer than 2012 to be wholesaled after 60 days. Open **AASFebTradeIns** and then save it with the name **2-AASFebTradeIns**. Insert formulas in column G that add 45 days to the date in column B for trade-ins 2012 and older and that add 60 days to trade-ins 2013 and newer. (If you know how, use an IF function in the formula so that the formula can be copied with the fill handle.) Apply the Short Date format to the range G4:G20. Save, print, and then close the workbook.

Part 4

The sales manager for Allenmore Auto Sales has asked you to find at least two websites that provide estimates of the value of used automobiles (such as Kelley Blue Book [kbb.com] and Edmunds.com). She wants you to add at least two hyperlinks to the February trade-ins workbook. Sales people can use the hyperlinks in the workbook to quickly determine the value of a used automobile. Use the Help feature to learn how to create hyperlinks in Excel. Open the **2-AASFebTradeIns** workbook and then save it with the name **2-AASFebTradeIns2**. Add at least two hyperlinks to websites that provide estimates of the value of used automobiles. Save, print, and then close the workbook.

Formatting a Worksheet

 The online course includes additional review and assessment resources.

Skills Assessment

Assessment 1

Format a Sales Worksheet

1. Open **NSPSales** and then save it with the name **3-NSPSales**.
2. Change the width of column A to 14.00 characters.
3. Change the width of columns B through E to 10.00 characters.
4. Select row 2 and then insert a new row.
5. Merge and center the range A2:E2.
6. Type Sales Department in cell A2 and then press the Enter key.
7. Increase the height of row 1 to 33.00 points.
8. Increase the height of row 2 to 21.00 points.
9. Increase the height of row 3 to 18.00 points.
10. Make the following formatting changes to the worksheet:
    a. Make cell A1 active, change the font size to 18 points, and then apply bold formatting.
    b. Make cell A2 active, change the font size to 14 points, and then apply bold formatting.
    c. Select the range A3:E3, apply bold formatting, and then click the Center button in the Alignment group.
    d. Select the range A1:E3 and then change the vertical alignment to *Middle Align*.
11. Insert the following formulas in the worksheet:
    a. Insert a formula in cell D4 that adds the amounts in cells B4 and C4. Copy the formula to the range D5:D11.
    b. Insert a formula in cell E4 that averages the amounts in cells B4 and C4. Copy the formula to the range E5:E11.
12. Make the following changes to the worksheet:
    a. Select the range B4:E4 and then apply the Accounting format with a dollar symbol ($) and no digits after the decimal point.
    b. Select the range B5:E11, apply the Comma format, and then change the number of digits after the decimal point to 0.
    c. Apply the Facet theme to the worksheet.
    d. Add a double-line border around the range A1:E11. *Hint: Use the **More Borders** option at the Borders button drop down list and then use options at the Format Cells dialog box with the Border tab selected to apply a double-line border to the outside of the selected range.*

e. Select cells A1 and A2 and then apply the Blue-Gray, Text 2, Lighter 80% fill color (fourth column, second row in the *Theme Colors* section).

f. Select the range A3:E3 and then apply the Blue-Gray, Text 2, Lighter 60% fill color (fourth column, third row in the *Theme Colors* section).

13. Save, print, and then close **3-NSPSales**.

Assessment 2

Format an Overdue Accounts Worksheet

1. Open **CCorpAccts** and then save it with the name **3-CCorpAccts**.
2. Change the widths of columns as follows:
   Column A: 21.00 characters
   Column B: 10.00 characters
   Column C: 12.00 characters
   Column D: 13.00 characters
   Column E: 7.00 characters
   Column F: 12.00 characters
3. Make cell A1 active and then insert a new row.
4. Merge and center the range A1:F1.
5. Type Compass Corporation in cell A1 and then press the Enter key.
6. Increase the height of row 1 to 42.00 points.
7. Increase the height of row 2 to 24.00 points.
8. Make the following formatting changes to the worksheet:
   a. Select the range A1:F11 and then change the font and font size to 10-point Cambria.
   b. Make cell A1 active, change the font size to 24 points, and then apply bold formatting.
   c. Make cell A2 active, change the font size to 18 points, and then apply bold formatting.
   d. Select the range A3:F3, apply bold formatting, and then click the Center button in the Alignment group.
   e. Select cell A1 and then click the Middle Align button.
   f. Select the range B4:B11 and then click the Center button.
   g. Select the range E4:E11 and then click the Center button.
9. Enter a formula in cell F4 that inserts the due date (the purchase date plus the number of days in the *Terms* column). Copy the formula to the range F5:F11.
10. Apply the following borders and fill color:
    a. Add a thick outside border around the range A1:F11.
    b. Make cell A2 active and then add a double-line border at the top and bottom of the cell.
    c. Select the range A3:F3 and then add a single-line border to the bottoms of the cells.
    d. Select cells A1 and A2 and then apply the Blue, Accent 1, Lighter 80% fill color (fifth column, second row in the *Theme Colors* section).
11. Save, print, and then close **3-CCorpAccts**.

Assessment 3

Format a Supplies and Equipment Worksheet

1. Open **OEBudget** and then save it with the name **3-OEBudget**.
2. Select and then merge the range A1:D2. *Hint: Use the* **Merge Across** *option at the* **Merge & Center** *button drop-down list*.
3. With cells A1 and A2 selected, click the Middle Align button in the Alignment group and then click the Center button.
4. Make cell A1 active and then change the font size to 22 points and apply bold formatting.

5. Make cell A2 active and then change the font size to 12 points and apply bold formatting.
6. Change the height of row 1 to 36.00 points.
7. Change the height of row 2 to 21.00 points.
8. Change the width of column A to 15.00 characters.
9. Select the range A3:A17, apply bold formatting, and then click the Wrap Text button in the Alignment group.
10. Make cell B3 active and then apply the Currency format with no digits after the decimal point.
11. Select the range C6:C19 and then apply the Percentage format with one digit after the decimal point.
12. Make cell D6 active and then type a formula that multiplies the absolute cell reference B3 with the percentage in cell C6. Copy the formula to the range D7:D19.
13. With the range D6:D19 selected and with the Currency format applied, format the numbers with no digits after the decimal point.
14. Make cell D8 active and then clear its contents. Use the Repeat command, the F4 function key, to clear the contents from cells D11, D14, and D17.
15. Select the range A1:D19, change the font to Constantia, and then change the font color to standard dark blue.
16. Add the Green, Accent 6, Lighter 80% fill color (last column, second row in the *Theme Colors* section) to the following cells: A1, A2, A5:D5, A8:D8, A11:D11, A14:D14, and A17:D17.
17. Automatically adjust the width of column B.
18. Save, print, and then close **3-OEBudget**.

Assessment 4

Format a Financial Analysis Worksheet

1. At a blank workbook, display the Format Cells dialog box with the Alignment tab selected and then experiment with the options in the *Text alignment* section and the *Text control* section. Click the Cancel button to close the dialog box.
2. Open **FinAnalysis** and then save it with the name **3-FinAnalysis**.
3. Make cell B9 active and then insert a formula that averages the percentages in the range B3:B8. Copy the formula to C9 and D9.
4. Select the range B3:D9, display the Format Cells dialog box with the Alignment tab selected, change the horizontal alignment to *Right (Indent)* and the indent to *2*, and then click OK.
5. Select the range A1:D9 and then change the font size to 14 points.
6. Select the range B2:D2 and then change the orientation to 45 degrees.
7. Automatically adjust the height of row 2.
8. Save, print, and then close **3-FinAnalysis**.

Visual Benchmark

Create a Worksheet and Insert Formulas

1. At a blank workbook, type the data in the cells as indicated in Figure 3.1 but *do not* type the data in the following ranges of cells: B8:D8, B14:D14, B20:D20, B22:D22, and B25:D25. For these cells, enter the appropriate formulas so the results match what you see in the figure. Calculate estimated gross profit by multiplying the *TOTAL* by the *Gross Profit Factor* (include an absolute reference so that the *Gross Profit Factor* cell reference stays the same when the formula is copied).
2. Apply formatting so your worksheet looks similar to the one shown in Figure 3.1.
3. Save the workbook and name it **3-BTBookings**.
4. Print **3-BTBookings**.
5. Turn on the display of formulas and then print the worksheet again.
6. Turn off the display of formulas and then close the workbook.

Figure 3.1 Visual Benchmark

	A	B	C	D
1		**Bayside Travel**		
2		**First Quarter Booking Totals**		
3		January	February	March
4	**Los Angeles**			
5	Tours	$ 65,395	$ 62,103	$ 58,450
6	Cruises	48,525	43,218	54,055
7	Other	29,329	26,398	30,391
8	**Total**	143,249	131,719	142,896
9				
10	**San Francisco**			
11	Tours	41,438	39,493	56,461
12	Cruises	23,147	18,530	40,530
13	Other	18,642	14,320	17,305
14	**Total**	83,227	72,343	114,296
15				
16	**Toronto**			
17	Tours	50,229	42,519	52,403
18	Cruises	49,260	41,490	39,230
19	Other	31,322	21,579	27,430
20	**Total**	130,811	105,588	119,063
21				
22	TOTAL	$ 357,287	$ 309,650	$ 376,255
23				
24	**Gross Profit Factor**	26%		
25	**Estimated Gross Profit**	$ 92,895	$ 80,509	$ 97,826
26				

Case Study

You are the office manager for HealthWise Fitness Center and have decided to prepare an Excel worksheet that shows the various plans offered by the health club. In this worksheet, you want to include yearly dues for each plan as well as quarterly and monthly payments. Open **HFCDues** and then save it with the name **3-HFCDues-1**. Make the following changes to the worksheet:

- Select the range B3:D8 and then apply the Accounting format with two digits after the decimal point and without dollar symbols.
- Make cell B3 active and then type 500.
- Make cell B4 active and then insert a formula that adds the amount in cell B3 with the product (multiplication) of cell B3 and 10%. (The formula should look like this: =B3+(B3*10%). The Economy plan is the base plan and each additional plan costs 10% more than the previous plan.)
- Copy the formula in cell B4 to the range B5:B8.
- Insert a formula in cell C3 that divides the amount in cell B3 by 4 and then copy the formula to the range C4:C8.
- Insert a formula in cell D3 that divides the amount in cell B3 by 12 and then copy the formula to the range D4:D8.
- Apply formatting to enhance the appearance of the worksheet.

Save and then print the completed worksheet.

With **3-HFCDues-1** open, save it with the name **3-HFCDues-2** and then make the following changes:

- You have been informed that the base rate for yearly dues has increased from $500.00 to $600.00. Change this amount in cell B3 of the worksheet.
- If clients are late with their quarterly or monthly dues payments, a late fee is charged. You decide to add the late fee information to the worksheet. Insert a new column to the right of column C. Type Late Fees in cell D2 and in cell F2.
- Insert a formula in cell D3 that multiplies the amount in C3 by 5%. Copy this formula to the range D4:D8.
- Insert a formula in cell F3 that multiplies the amount in cell E3 by 7%. Copy this formula to the range F4:F8. If necessary, apply the Accounting format to the range F3:F8 with two digits after the decimal point and without dollar symbols.
- Select the range B3:F3 and change the Accounting format to include dollar symbols.
- Select the range B8:F8 and change the Accounting format to include dollar symbols.
- Apply formatting to enhance the visual appearance of the worksheet.

Save, print, and then close **3-HFCDues-2**.

Part 2

Prepare a payroll sheet for the employees of HealthWise Fitness Center using the information in Figure 3.2. Include the following information:

Insert a formula in the *Overtime Pay* column that multiplies the hourly wage by the overtime rate, which is 1.5, and then multiplies that amount by the number of overtime hours. (Include parentheses around the first part of the formula.)

Insert a formula in the *Weekly Salary* column that multiplies the hourly wage by the number of hours and then adds the overtime pay. (Include parentheses around the first part of the formula.)

Apply formatting to enhance the appearance of the worksheet. Save the workbook and name it **3-HFCPayroll**. Turn on the display of formulas, print the worksheet, and then turn off the display of formulas.

Make the following changes to the worksheet:

- Change the hourly wage for Amanda Turney to $22.00.
- Increase the hours for Daniel Joyner to 20 hours.
- Remove the row for Grant Baker.
- Insert a row between Jean Overmeyer and Bonnie Haddon and then type the following information in the cells in the new row: *Employee:* McGuire, Tonya; *Hourly Wage:* $17.50; *Hours:* 15; *Overtime Hours:* 0.

Save and then print **3-HFCPayroll**. Turn on the display of formulas, print the worksheet again, and then turn off the display of formulas. Save and then close **3-HFCPayroll**.

Figure 3.2 Case Study Part 2

HealthWise Fitness Center					
Weekly Payroll					
Employee	Hourly Wage	Hours	Overtime Hours	Overtime Pay	Weekly Salary
Heaton, Kelly	$26.50	40	2		
Severson, Joel	$25.00	40	0		
Turney, Amanda	$20.00	15	0		
Walters, Leslie	$19.65	30	0		
Overmeyer, Jean	$18.00	20	0		
Haddon, Bonnie	$16.00	40	3		
Baker, Grant	$15.00	40	0		
Calveri, Shannon	$12.00	15	0		
Dugan, Emily	$10.50	40	4		
Joyner, Daniel	$10.50	10	0		
Lee, Alexander	$10.50	10	0		

Part

3

The manager of HealthWise Fitness Center is interested in ordering new equipment for the health club. She would like to order three elliptical machines, three recumbent bikes, and three upright bikes. She has asked you to use the internet to research models and prices for this new equipment and then prepare a worksheet with the information. Using the internet, search for information about the following equipment:

- Search for elliptical machines for sale. Locate two different models and, if possible, find at least two companies that sell each model. Record the company names, model numbers, and prices.
- Search for recumbent bikes for sale. Locate two different models and, if possible, find at least two companies that sell each model. Record the company names, model numbers, and prices.
- Search for upright bikes for sale. Locate two different models and, if possible, find at least two companies that sell each model. Record the company names, model numbers, and prices.

Using the information you found, prepare an Excel worksheet with the following information:

- Company name
- Equipment name
- Equipment model
- Price
- A column that multiplies the price by the number required (which is 3)

Add the fitness center name, HealthWise Fitness Center, and any other information you think is necessary to the worksheet. Apply formatting to enhance the appearance of the worksheet. Save the workbook and name it **3-HFCEquip**. Print and then close **3-HFCEquip**.

Part

4

When a prospective client contacts HealthWise Fitness Center about joining, you send a letter containing information about the fitness center, the plans offered, and the dues amounts. Use a letter template in Word to create a letter to send to a prospective client. (You determine the client's name and address.) Copy the cells in **3-HFCDues-2** containing data and then paste them into the body of the letter. Make formatting changes to make the data readable. Save the document and name it **3-HFCLetter**. Print and then close **3-HFCLetter**.

Enhancing a Worksheet

 The online content includes additional review and assessment resources.

Skills Assessment

Assessment

1

Format a Data Analysis Worksheet

1. Open **DISemiSales** and then save it with the name **4-DISemiSales**.
2. Make the following changes to the worksheet:
   a. Insert a formula in cell H4 that averages the amounts in the range B4:G4.
   b. Copy the formula in cell H4 to the range H5:H9.
   c. Insert a formula in cell B10 that adds the amounts in the range B4:B9.
   d. Copy the formula in cell B10 to the range C10:H10. (Click the Auto Fill Options button and then click *Fill Without Formatting* at the drop-down list.)
   e. Apply the Accounting format to cell H4.
   f. Change to landscape orientation.
   g. Change the top margin to 2.8 inches and the left margin to 1.3 inches.
3. Save and then print **4-DISemiSales**.
4. Make the following changes to the worksheet:
   a. Change back to portrait orientation.
   b. Change the top margin to 1 inch and the left margin to 0.7 inch.
   c. Horizontally and vertically center the worksheet on the page.
   d. Scale the worksheet so it fits on one page.
   e. Change the page size to A4.
5. Save, print, and then close **4-DISemiSales**.

Assessment

2

Format a Test Results Worksheet

1. Open **CMTests** and then save it with the name **4-CMTests**.
2. Make the following changes to the worksheet:
   a. Insert a formula in cell N4 that averages the test scores in the range B4:M4.
   b. Copy the formula in cell N4 to the range N5:N21.
   c. Type Average in cell A22.
   d. Insert a formula in cell B22 that averages the test scores in the range B4:B21.
   e. Copy the formula in cell B22 to the range C22:N22.
   f. Insert a page break between columns G and H.
3. View the worksheet using Page Break Preview.
4. Change back to the Normal view.
5. Specify that the column titles (A3 through A22) are to print on each page.
6. Create a header that prints the page number at the right of the page.

7. Create a footer that prints your name at the left of the page and the workbook file name at the right of the page.
8. Display the worksheet in Normal view.
9. Save and then print the worksheet.
10. Set a print area for the range N3:N22 and then print these cells.
11. Clear the print area.
12. Save and then close **4-CMTests**.

Assessment

3

Format an Equipment Rental Worksheet

1. Open **HERInvoices** and then save it with the name **4-HERInvoices**.
2. Insert a formula in cell H3 that multiplies the rate in cell G3 by the hours in cell F3. Copy the formula in cell H3 to the range H4:H16.
3. Insert a formula in cell H17 that sums the amounts in the range H3:H16.
4. Complete the following finds and replaces:
   a. Find all occurrences of *75* and replace them with *90*.
   b. Find all occurrences of *55* and replace them with *60*.
   c. Find all occurrences of *Barrier Concrete* and replace them with *Lee Sand and Gravel*.
   d. Find all occurrences of 11-point Calibri and replace them with 10-point Cambria.
   e. After completing the finds and replaces, clear all formatting from the Format buttons.
5. Insert a header that prints the date in the left header box and the time in the right header box.
6. Insert a footer that prints your name in the left footer box and the workbook file name in the right footer box.
7. Horizontally and vertically center the worksheet on the page.
8. Change the orientation to landscape.
9. Change the page size to letter.
10. Save, print, and then close **4-HERInvoices**.

Assessment

4

Format an Invoices Worksheet

1. Open **RPInvoices** and then save it with the name **4-RPInvoices**.
2. Insert a formula in cell G4 that multiplies the amount in cell E4 by the percentage in cell F4 and then adds the product to the amount in cell E4. (If you write the formula correctly, the result in cell G4 will display as *$488.25*.)
3. Copy the formula in cell G4 to the range G5:G17, click the Auto Fill Options button, and then click the *Fill Without Formatting* option.
4. Complete a spelling check on the worksheet.
5. Find all occurrences of *Picture* and replace them with *Portrait*. (Do not press the spacebar after typing Picture or Portrait in the *Find what text* box because you also want to find occurrences of each word that end with an *s*. Make sure the *Match entire cell contents* check box does not contain a check mark.)
6. Sort the records by invoice number in ascending order (smallest to largest).
7. Complete a new sort that sorts the records by client number in ascending order (A to Z).
8. Complete a custom sort that sorts by date in ascending order (oldest to newest) and then by amount in descending order (largest to smallest).
9. Insert a footer in the worksheet that prints your name in the left footer box and the current date in the right footer box.
10. Display the worksheet in Normal view.

11. Center the worksheet horizontally and vertically on the page.
12. Save and then print **4-RPInvoices**.
13. Select the range A3:G3 and then turn on the filter feature and complete the following filters:
    a. Filter and then print a list of rows containing client number 11-279 and then clear the filter.
    b. Filter and then print a list of rows containing the three highest amounts due and then clear the filter.
    c. Filter and then print a list of rows containing amounts due that are less than $500 and then clear the filter.
14. Save and then close **4-RPInvoices**.

Assessment 5 — Create a Worksheet Containing Keyboard Shortcuts

1. Use Excel's Help feature to learn about keyboard shortcuts in Excel. After reading the information presented, create a worksheet with the following features:
   - Create a title for the worksheet.
   - Include at least 10 keyboard shortcuts along with an explanation of each shortcut.
   - Set the data in cells in a typeface other than Calibri and change the data color.
   - Add borders to the cells. (You determine the border style.)
   - Add a fill color to cells. (You determine the color; make it complement the data color.)
   - Create a header that prints the date at the right margin and create a footer that prints your name at the left margin and the file name at the right margin.
2. Save the workbook and name it **4-KeyboardShortcuts**.
3. Print and then close **4-KeyboardShortcuts**.

Visual Benchmark

Create and Format an Expense Worksheet

1. At a blank workbook, type the data in the cells as indicated in Figure 4.1 on the next page but **do not** type the data in the cells noted below. Instead, insert the formulas as indicated:
   - In the range N3:N8, insert a formula that sums the monthly expenses for the year.
   - In the range B9:N9, insert a formula that sums the monthly expenses for each month and the entire year.
   (The results of your formulas should match the results you see in the figure.)
2. Change the left and right margins to 0.45 inch and change the top margin to 1.5 inches.
3. Apply formatting so your worksheet looks similar to the one shown in Figure 4.1. (Set the heading in 26-point Cambria and set the remaining data in 10-point Cambria. Apply bold formatting as shown in the figure.)
4. Save the workbook and name it **4-HERExpenses**.

5. Look at the printing of the worksheet shown in Figure 4.2 and then make the following changes:
   - Insert a page break between columns G and H.
   - Insert the headers and footer as shown.
   - Specify that the column titles print on the second page, as shown in Figure 4.2.
6. Save and then print **4-HERExpenses**. (Your worksheet should print on two pages and appear as shown in Figure 4.2.)
7. Close **4-HERExpenses**.

Figure 4.1 Visual Benchmark Data

	A	B	C	D	E	F	G	H	I	J	K	L	M	N
1						Hilltop Equipment Rental								
2	Expenses	January	February	March	April	May	June	July	August	September	October	November	December	Total
3	Lease	$ 3,250	$ 3,250	$ 3,250	$ 3,250	$ 3,250	$ 3,250	$ 3,250	$ 3,250	$ 3,250	$ 3,250	$ 3,250	$ 3,250	$ 39,000
4	Utilities	3,209	2,994	2,987	2,500	2,057	1,988	1,845	1,555	1,890	2,451	2,899	3,005	29,380
5	Payroll	10,545	9,533	11,542	10,548	11,499	12,675	13,503	13,258	12,475	10,548	10,122	9,359	135,607
6	Insurance	895	895	895	895	895	895	895	895	895	895	895	895	10,740
7	Maintenance	2,439	1,856	2,455	5,410	3,498	3,110	2,479	3,100	1,870	6,105	4,220	3,544	40,086
8	Supplies	341	580	457	330	675	319	451	550	211	580	433	601	5,528
9	Total Expenses	$ 20,679	$ 19,108	$ 21,586	$ 22,933	$ 21,874	$ 22,237	$ 22,423	$ 22,608	$ 20,591	$ 23,829	$ 21,819	$ 20,654	$ 260,341

Figure 4.2 Visual Benchmark Printed Pages

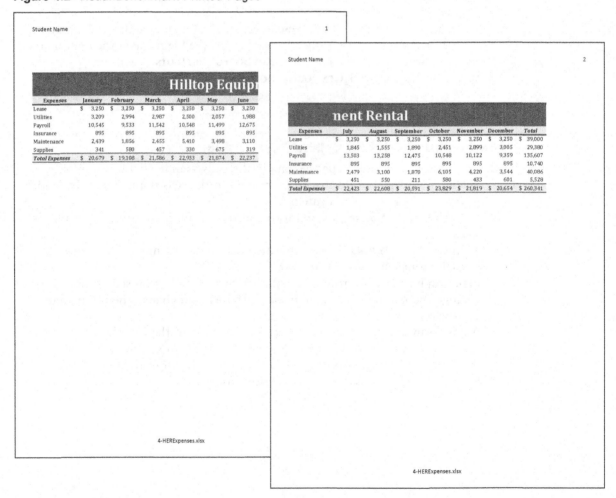

Case Study

You are a sales associate for Macadam Realty. Your supervisor has asked you to complete a form she started that contains information on sample mortgages. She wants to make the form available in the reception area display rack. She has already inserted a formula (in cell G4) that calculates monthly payments using the PMT function. (You will learn more about this function in Chapter 6.) Open **MRMortgages** and then save it with the name **4-MRMortgages-01**. Add the following information and make the following changes:

- In column C, insert a formula that determines the down payment amount. Copy the formula in cell C4 to the range C5:C47.
- In column D, insert a formula that determines the loan amount. Copy the formula in cell C4 to the range D5:D47.
- In column G, drag the formula in cell G4 to the range G5:G47.
- Insert the date and time as a header and your name and the workbook name (**4-MRMortgages-01**) as a footer.
- Find 11-point Calibri formatting and replace it with 11-point Candara formatting. After completing the find and replace, clear all formatting from the Format buttons.
- Scale the worksheet so it prints on one page.

Save and then print **4-MRMortgages-01**. After looking at the printed worksheet, you decide to make the following changes:

- Sort the values in the *Price of Home* column from smallest to largest.
- Change the percentage amount in column E from 6% to 7%.
- Shade the cells in row 4 that contain data in the light-gold color that matches the fill in cell A2. Copy this shading to every other row of cells in the worksheet (stopping at row 46).
- Apply the Accounting format with a dollar symbol ($) and no digits after the decimal point to cells A4, C4, D4, and G4.

Save the edited worksheet with Save As and name it **4-MRMortgages-02**. Make sure the worksheet prints on one page. Save, print, and then close **4-MRMortgages-02**.

In your position at Macadam Realty, you are responsible for preparing a worksheet that contains sales and commissions for the year. You will print the worksheet for distribution to staff members who will be attending an upcoming meeting. You have created the worksheet and included the sales and commission totals and now need to insert formulas and format the worksheet. Open **MRSalesComms** and then save it with the name **4-MRSalesComms**. Make the following changes to the worksheet:

- Calculate the sales and commissions and insert the totals in the appropriate locations in the worksheet.
- Calculate the total sales and total commissions and insert the totals in the appropriate locations in the worksheet.
- Apply appropriate number formatting.
- Apply formatting so the worksheet is formatted similarly to the worksheet you prepared in Part 1.
- Change the top margin to 3 inches.
- Include a header that prints the page number and a footer that prints your name.

Save the worksheet and then print it so that the column titles (A4:A17) print on all pages. After looking at the worksheet, you decide to make the following changes:

- Remove the column titles from printing on each page.
- Remove the header containing the page number.
- Edit the footer so the date prints at the left margin and your name prints at the right margin.
- Change to landscape orientation.
- Change the top margin to 2.5 inches.
- Scale the worksheet so it prints on one page.

Save, print, and then close **4-MRSalesComms**.

Part
3

As a sales associate at Macadam Realty, you have Canadian clients that are interested in purchasing real estate in the United States. For those clients, you like to keep a dollar conversion worksheet available. Using the internet, search for a site that converts US dollars to Canadian dollars. Determine the current currency exchange rate and then create a worksheet with the following specifications:

- Apply formatting that is similar to the formatting in the worksheets you worked with in Parts 1 and 2 of the case study.
- Create a column for home prices in US dollars with amounts that begin with $100,000, increase by increments of $50,000, and end with $1,000,000.
- Create a column for home prices converted to Canadian dollars. (Insert a formula in the column that converts the US dollar amounts for home prices to Canadian dollars.)
- Apply any other formatting you feel will improve the appearance of the worksheet.

Save the completed workbook and name it **4-CanadaPrices**. Display formulas and then print the worksheet. Turn off the display of formulas and then save and close the workbook.

Microsoft® Excel Level 1

Unit 1 Performance Assessment

Data Files

Before beginning unit work, copy the EL1U1 folder to your storage medium and then make EL1U1 the active folder.

Assessing Proficiency

In this unit, you have learned to create, save, print, edit, and format Excel worksheets; create and insert formulas; sort and filter data; and enhance worksheets with features such as headers, footers, and page numbering.

Assessment
1

Calculate Total, Maximum, Minimum, and Average Yearly Sales

1. Open **DISales** and then save it with the name **U1-DISales**.
2. Insert in the range D4:D14 the appropriate sales totals.
3. Insert in cells B15, C15, and D15 the appropriate first-half, second-half, and total sales, respectively.
4. Insert in cell B17 a formula that inserts the maximum total sales amount from the range D4:D14.
5. Insert in cell B18 a formula that inserts the minimum total sales amount from the range D4:D14.
6. Insert in cell B19 a formula that inserts the average of total sales in the range D4:D14.
7. Apply the Accounting format to cell D4 with a dollar symbol ($). (Make sure there are no digits after the decimal point.)
8. Save, print, and then close **U1-DISales**.

Assessment
2

Create a Worksheet with AutoFill and Calculate Total Hours and Gross Pay

1. Create the Excel worksheet shown in Figure U1.1. Use AutoFill to fill in the days of the week and some of the hours. (Consider using Alt + Enter, when necessary to wrap text in the column headings as shown in the figure.)
2. Insert a SUM function in the range H4:H10 that calculates the total hours.
3. Insert a formula in the range J4:J10 that calculates the gross pay (total hours multiplied by pay rate).

4. Insert a formula in the range B11:J11 that calculates the totals of the hours for each day of the week as well as total hours, pay rate, and gross pay.
5. Apply formatting to the cells as shown in the figure.
6. Change the page orientation to landscape.
7. Save the worksheet and name it **U1-CPPayroll**.
8. Turn on the display of formulas, print the worksheet (prints on two pages), and then turn off the display of formulas.
9. Save and then close **U1-CPPayroll**.

Figure U1.1 Assessment 2

	A	B	C	D	E	F	G	H	I	J
1				**Capstan Products**						
2				Payroll - Week Ended: March 13, 2021						
3	**Employee**	**Monday**	**Tuesday**	**Wednesday**	**Thursday**	**Friday**	**Saturday**	**Total Hours**	**Pay Rate**	**Gross Pay**
4	Loftus, Maureen	8	8	8	8	8	0	40	$ 28.50	$ 1,140.00
5	Banyai, Robert	3	3	3	3	0	8	20	15.35	307.00
6	Martinez, Michelle	0	8	8	8	8	8	40	19.00	760.00
7	Wilhelm, Marshall	0	5	5	5	5	8	28	13.50	378.00
8	Ziegler, Cathleen	0	0	0	0	4	4	8	22.45	179.60
9	Hope, Trevor	0	0	0	0	4	4	8	13.50	108.00
10	Anthony, Charles	0	4	4	4	4	4	20	13.50	270.00
11	**Total**	11	28	28	28	33	36	164	$ 125.80	$ 3,142.60
12										

Assessment 3

Create a Sales Bonus Workbook

1. Create the Excel worksheet shown in Figure U1.2. Format the cells to match how they appear in the figure.
2. Insert a formula in the range D4:D11 that calculates the bonus amount (sales multiplied by bonus percentage).
3. Insert a formula in the range E4:E11 that calculates the net sales (sales minus bonus amount).
4. Insert the sum of the values in the range B4:B11 in cell B12, the sum of the values in the range D4:D11 in cell D12, and the sum of the values in the range E4:E11 in cell E12.
5. Apply the Comma format with no digits after the decimal point to the range B5:B11 and the range D5:E11.
6. Apply the Accounting format with a dollar symbol and no digits after the decimal point to cells B4, D4, E4, B12, D12, and E12.
7. Insert a footer with your first and last names in the left footer box and the current date in the right footer box.
8. Print the worksheet centered horizontally and vertically on the page.
9. Save the workbook and name it **U1-SBASales**.
10. Close **U1-SBASales**.

Assessment 4

Format a Department Budget

1. Open **CMBudgets** and then save it with the name **U1-CMBudgets**.
2. Insert a formula in cell C5:C12 using an absolute cell reference to determine the projected budget with an increase of 10% over the current budget. (Use the number *1.1* in cell B3 when writing the formula.) Copy the formula to C6:C12.

3. Insert formulas to total the budget amounts and the projected budget amounts.
4. Make cell A15 active and then use the NOW function to insert the current date and time.
5. Save and then print the worksheet.
6. Determine the projected budget with an increase of 5% over the current budget by changing the text in cell A3 to *5% Increase* and the number in cell B3 to *1.05*.
7. Apply the Wisp theme and then apply the Median theme colors.
8. Save, print, and then close **U1-CMBudgets**.

Figure U1.2 Assessment 3

	A	B	C	D	E
1		Stanton & Barnet Associates			
2		Sales Department			
3	Associate	Sales	Bonus	Bonus Amount	Net Sales
4	Conway, Amanda	$ 101,450	5%		
5	Eckhart, Geneva	94,375	2%		
6	Farris, Edward	73,270	0%		
7	Greenwood, Wayne	110,459	5%		
8	Hagen, Chandra	120,485	5%		
9	Logan, Courtney	97,520	2%		
10	Pena, Geraldo	115,850	5%		
11	Rubin, Alex	76,422	0%		
12	Total				
13					

Assessment 5

Format a Weekly Payroll Workbook

1. Open **CCPayroll** and then save it with the name **U1-CCPayroll**.
2. Insert a formula in cell E3 that multiplies the hourly rate by the hours and then adds that amount to the product (multiplication) of the hourly rate by the overtime pay rate (1.5) by the overtime hours. (Use parentheses in the formula and use an absolute cell reference for the overtime pay rate. Refer to Chapter 2, Activity 3c.) Copy the formula to the range E4:E16.
3. Insert a formula in cell F3 that multiplies the gross pay by the withholding tax rate (W/H Rate). (Use an absolute cell reference for the cell containing the withholding rate. Refer to Chapter 2, Activity 3c.) Copy the formula to the range F4:F16.
4. Insert a formula in cell G3 that multiplies the gross pay by the social security rate (SS Rate). (Use an absolute cell reference for the cell containing the social security rate. Refer to Chapter 2, Activity 3c.) Copy the formula to the range G4:G16.
5. Insert a formula in cell H3 that adds the social security tax and the withholding tax and then subtracts that sum from the gross pay. (Refer to Chapter 2, Activity 3c.) Copy the formula to the range H4:H16.
6. Sort the employee last names alphabetically in ascending order (A to Z).

7. Center the worksheet horizontally and vertically on the page.
8. Apply the Retrospect theme and then apply the Blue Green theme colors.
9. Adjust column A to 18.00 points.
10. Insert a header with your name in the left header box and the file name in the right header box.
11. Save, print, and then close **U1-CCPayroll**.

Assessment 6

Format a Customer Sales Analysis Workbook

1. Open **DIAnnualSales** and then save it with the name **U1-DIAnnualSales**.
2. Insert formulas and copy formulas to complete the worksheet.
3. Insert in cell B11 the highest total from the range B10:M10. Insert in cell B12 the lowest total from the range B10:M10.
4. Change the orientation to landscape.
5. Insert a page break between columns G and H.
6. Insert a header with the page number in the right header box.
7. Insert a footer with your name in the right footer box.
8. Center the worksheet horizontally and vertically on the page.
9. Specify that the row headings in the range A3:A12 print on both pages.
10. Save, print, and then close **U1-DIAnnualSales**.

Assessment 7

Format an Invoices Workbook

1. Open **RPInvoices** and then save it with the name **U1-RPInvoices**.
2. Insert a formula in cell G4 that multiplies the amount in cell E4 by the percentage in cell F4 and then adds that amount to the amount in cell E4.
3. Copy the formula in cell G4 to the range G5:G18.
4. Apply the Accounting format with two digits after the decimal point and a dollar symbol to cell G4. Apply the Comma format with two digits after the decimal point to the range G5:G18.
5. Find all occurrences of *11-279* and replace them with *10-005*.
6. Find all occurrences of *8.5* and replace them with *9.0*.
7. Find all occurrences of the Calibri font and replace them with the Candara font. (Do not specify a type size so Excel replaces all sizes of Calibri with Candara.) After completing the find and replace, clear all formatting from the Format buttons.
8. Print **U1-RPInvoices**.
9. Filter and then print a list of rows that contain only the client number *04-325*. (After printing, return the list to *(Select All)*.)
10. Filter and then print a list of rows that contain only the service *Development*. (After printing, return the list to *(Select All)*.)
11. Filter and then print a list of rows that contain the three highest totals in the *Amount Due* column. (After printing, turn off the filter feature.)
12. Save and then close **U1-RPInvoices**.

Writing Activities

The following activities give you the opportunity to practice your writing skills and demonstrate your understanding of some of the important Excel features you have mastered in this unit. Use correct grammar, appropriate word choices, and clear sentence construction.

Plan and Prepare an Orders Summary Workbook

Plan and prepare a worksheet with the information shown in Figure U1.3. Apply formatting of your choosing. Save the completed worksheet and name it **U1-OrdersSumm**. Print and then close **U1-OrdersSumm**.

Figure U1.3 Activity 1

Prepare a weekly summary of orders taken that itemizes the products coming into the company and the average order size. The products, order amounts, and average order sizes are as follows:

Black and gold wall clock: $2,450 worth of orders, average order size of 125 units

Traveling alarm clock: $1,358 worth of orders, average order size of 195 units

Waterproof watch: $890 worth of orders, average order size of 90 units

Dashboard clock: $2,135 worth of orders, average order size of 230 units

Pyramid clock: $3,050 worth of orders, average order size of 375 units

Gold chain watch: $755 worth of orders, average order size of 80 units

In the worksheet, calculate the price per unit for each item and total the amount of the orders. Sort the data in the worksheet by the order amount in descending order.

Prepare a Depreciation Workbook

Assets within a company, such as equipment, can be depreciated over time. Several methods are available for determining the amount of depreciation, such as the straight-line depreciation method, the fixed-declining balance method, and the double-declining method. Use Excel's Help feature to learn about two depreciation methods: straight-line and double-declining depreciation. (The straight-line depreciation function, SLN, and the double-declining depreciation function, DDB, are in the *Financial* category.) After reading about the two methods, create an Excel worksheet that describes the methods with the following information:

- An appropriate title
- A heading for straight-line depreciation
- The straight-line depreciation function
- The name of and a description of each straight-line depreciation function argument category
- A heading for double-declining depreciation
- The double-declining depreciation function
- The name of and a description of each double-declining depreciation function argument category

Apply formatting of your choosing to the worksheet. Save the completed workbook and name it **U1-DepMethods**. Print the worksheet centered horizontally and vertically on the page. Close **U1-DepMethods**.

Activity

3

Insert a Straight-Line Depreciation Formula

Open **RPDepreciation** and then save it with the name **U1-RPDepreciation**. Insert the function to determine straight-line depreciation in cell E4. Copy the formula to the range E5:E9. Print the worksheet centered horizontally and vertically on the page. Save and then close **U1-RPDepreciation**.

Optional: Briefly research straight-line and double-declining depreciation to find out why businesses depreciate their assets. What purpose does it serve? Locate information about the topics on the internet. Then use Word to write a half-page, single-spaced report explaining the financial reasons for using depreciation methods. Save the document and name it **U1-DepReport**. Print and then close the document.

Internet Research

Create a Travel Planning Worksheet

Search online for information about traveling to a country that interests you. Find sites that provide cost information for airfare, hotels, meals, entertainment, and car rentals. Using the first week of the next month as the travel dates, create a planning worksheet for a trip to that country that includes the following:

- An appropriate title
- Appropriate headings
- Round-trip airfare costs
- Hotel or vacation rental costs (off-season and in-season rates if available)
- Estimated meal costs
- Entertainment costs
- Car rental costs

Save the completed workbook and name it **U1-TrvlWksht**. Print and then close the workbook.

Microsoft Excel Level 1

Unit 2

Enhancing the Display of Workbooks

Moving Data within and between Workbooks

 The online course includes additional review and assessment resources.

Skills Assessment

Assessment

1

Copy and Paste Data between Worksheets in a Sales Workbook

1. Open **EPSales** and then save it with the name **5-EPSales**.
2. Turn on the display of the Clipboard task pane, click the Clear All button to clear any content, and then complete the following steps:
   a. Select and copy the range A7:C7.
   b. Select and copy the range A10:C10.
   c. Select and copy the range A13:C13.
   d. Display the second worksheet, make cell A7 active, and then paste the *Avalon Clinic* cells.
   e. Make cell A10 active and then paste the *Stealth Media* cells.
   f. Make cell A13 active and then paste the *Danmark Contracting* cells.
   g. Make the third worksheet active and then complete similar steps to paste the cells in the same location as in the second worksheet.
   h. Clear the contents of the Clipboard task pane and then close the task pane.
3. Change the name of the Sheet1 tab to *2019 Sales*, the name of the Sheet2 tab to *2020 Sales*, and the name of the Sheet3 tab to *2021 Sales*.
4. Change the color of the 2019 Sales tab to standard blue, the color of the 2020 Sales tab to standard green, and the color of the 2021 Sales tab to standard yellow.
5. Make 2019 Sales the active worksheet, select all three tabs, and then insert a formula in cell D4 that sums the amounts in cells B4 and C4. Copy the formula in cell D4 to the range D5:D14.
6. Make cell D15 active and then insert a formula that sums the amounts in the range D4:D14.
7. To cell D4 in all three worksheets, apply the Accounting format with a dollar symbol ($) and no digits after the decimal point.
8. Insert a footer on all three worksheets that prints your name at the left and the current date at the right.
9. Save **5-EPSales**.
10. Print all three worksheets and then close **5-EPSales**.

Assessment 2

Copy, Paste, and Format Worksheets in an Income Statement Workbook

1. Open **CMJanIncome** and then save it with the name **5-CMJanIncome**.
2. Copy the range A1:B17 in Sheet1 and then paste the range into Sheet2. (Click the Paste Options button and then click the Keep Source Column Widths button in the Paste section at the drop-down list.)
3. Make the following changes to the Sheet2 worksheet:
   a. Adjust the row heights so they match the heights in the Sheet1 worksheet.
   b. Change the month from *January* to *February*.
   c. Change the amount in cell B4 to *97,655*.
   d. Change the amount in cell B5 to *39,558*.
   e. Change the amount in cell B11 to *1,105*.
4. Select both sheet tabs and then insert the following formulas:
   a. Insert a formula in cell B6 that subtracts the cost of sales from the sales revenue (*=b4-b5*).
   b. Insert a formula in cell B16 that sums the amounts in the range B8:B15.
   c. Insert a formula in cell B17 that subtracts the total expenses from the gross profit (*=b6-b16*).
5. Change the name of the Sheet1 tab to *January* and the name of the Sheet2 tab to *February*.
6. Change the color of the January tab to standard blue and the color of the February tab to standard red.
7. Insert custom headers on both worksheets that print your name at the left, the date in the middle, and the file name at the right.
8. Save, print, and then close **5-CMJanIncome**.

Assessment 3

Freeze and Unfreeze Window Panes in a Test Scores Workbook

1. Open **CMCertTests** and then save it with the name **5-CMCertTests**.
2. Make cell B3 active and then freeze the window panes.
3. Add two rows immediately above row 18 and then type the following text in the specified cells:

A18	Nauer, Sheryl	A19	Nunez, James
B18	75	B19	98
C18	83	C19	96
D18	85	D19	100
E18	78	E19	90
F18	82	F19	95
G18	80	G19	93
H18	79	H19	88
I18	82	I19	91
J18	92	J19	89
K18	90	K19	100
L18	86	L19	96
M18	84	M19	98

4. Insert a formula in cell N3 that averages the percentages in the range B3:M3 and then copy the formula to the range N4:N22.
5. Unfreeze the window panes.
6. Change to landscape orientation and then scale the worksheet to print on one page. *Hint: Do this with the* Width *option in the Scale to Fit group on the Page Layout tab.*
7. Save, print, and then close **5-CMCertTests**.

Assessment

4

Create, Copy, Paste, and Format Cells in an Equipment Usage Workbook

1. Create the worksheet shown in Figure 5.1. (Change the width of column A to 21.00 characters.)
2. Save the workbook and name it **5-HCMachRpt**.
3. With **5-HCMachRpt** open, open **HCEqpRpt**.
4. Select and copy the following cells from **HCEqpRpt** to **5-HCMachRpt**:
   a. Copy the range A4:G4 in **HCEqpRpt** and then paste the cells into **5-HCMachRpt** beginning with cell A12.
   b. Copy the range A10:G10 in **HCEqpRpt** and then paste the cells into **5-HCMachRpt** beginning with cell A13.
5. With **5-HCMachRpt** the active workbook, make cell A1 active and then apply the following formatting:
   a. Change the height of row 1 to 24.00 points.
   b. Change the font size of the text in cell A1 to 18 points.
   c. Apply the Blue, Accent 5, Lighter 80% fill color (ninth column, second row in the *Theme Colors* section) to cell A1.
6. Select the range A2:G2 and then apply the Blue, Accent 5, Darker 50% fill color (ninth column, last row in the *Theme Colors* section).
7. Select the range B2:G2 and then apply the White, Background 1 text color (first column, first row in the *Theme Colors* section). (Make sure the text in the cells is right-aligned.)
8. Select and then apply the Blue, Accent 5, Lighter 80% fill color (ninth column, second row in the *Theme Colors* section) to the following ranges of cells: A3:G3, A7:G7, and A11:G11.
9. Print the worksheet centered horizontally and vertically on the page.
10. Save and then close **5-HCMachRpt**.
11. Close **HCEqpRpt** without saving the changes.

Figure 5.1 Assessment 4

	A	B	C	D	E	F	G
1		EQUIPMENT USAGE REPORT					
2		January	February	March	April	May	June
3	Machine #12						
4	Total hours available	2200	2330	2430	2300	2340	2140
5	In use	1940	2005	2220	2080	1950	1895
6							
7	Machine #25						
8	Total hours available	2100	2240	2450	2105	2390	1950
9	In use	1800	1935	2110	1750	2215	1645
10							
11	Machine #30						

Copying and Linking Excel Data in a Word Document

1. In this chapter, you learned how to link data in cells between worksheets. You can also copy data in an Excel worksheet and then paste and link the data in a file in another program, such as Word. Use buttons at the Paste Options button drop-down list to link data or use options at the Paste Special dialog box. Open Word and then open the document **DWLtr**. Save the document with the name **5-DWLtr**.
2. Click the Excel button on the taskbar, open **DWMortgages**, and then save it with the name **5-DWMortgages**.
3. Select the range A2:G10 and then click the Copy button.
4. Click the Word button on the taskbar. (This displays **5-DWLtr**.)
5. Position the insertion point between the two paragraphs of text.
6. Click the Paste button arrow and then click *Paste Special* at the drop-down list.
7. At the Paste Special dialog box, look at the options available. Click the *Paste link* option, click *Microsoft Excel Worksheet Object* in the *As* list box, and then click OK.
8. Save, print, and then close **5-DWLtr**.
9. Click the Excel button on the taskbar.
10. Make cell A3 active and then change the number from *$300,000* to *$400,000*. Using the fill without formatting option, copy the number in cell A3 to the range A4:A10. (Cells in the range A3:A10 should contain the amount *$400,000*.)
11. Save, print, and then close **5-DWMortgages**.
12. Click the Word button on the taskbar.
13. Open **5-DWLtr**. At the message that displays asking if you want to update the data from the linked files, click Yes.
14. Change any instance of the amount *$300,000* in the first paragraph of text to *$400,000*.
15. Save, print, and then close **5-DWLtr**.
16. Close Word.

Visual Benchmark

Create and Format a Sales Worksheet Using Formulas

1. At a blank workbook, create the worksheet shown in Figure 5.2 with the following specifications:
   - Do not type the data in cells in the range D4:D9. Instead, enter a formula that totals the first-half and second-half yearly sales.
   - Apply the formatting shown in the figure, including changing font sizes, column widths, and row heights and inserting shading and border lines.
   - Rename the sheet tab and change the tab color as shown in the figure.
2. Copy the range A1:D9 and then paste the cells in Sheet2.
3. Edit the cells and apply formatting so the worksheet matches the worksheet shown in Figure 5.3. Rename the sheet tab and change the tab color as shown in the figure.
4. Save the completed workbook and name it **5-CMSemiSales**.
5. Print both worksheets.
6. Close **5-CMSemiSales**.

Figure 5.2 Visual Benchmark - Sales 2020 Worksheet

	A	B	C	D
1	**Clearline Manufacturing**			
2	SEMIANNUAL SALES - 2020			
3	Customer	1st Half	2nd Half	Total
4	Lakeside Trucking	$ 84,300	$ 73,500	$ 157,800
5	Gresham Machines	33,000	40,500	73,500
6	Real Photography	30,890	35,465	66,355
7	Genesis Productions	72,190	75,390	147,580
8	Landower Company	22,000	15,000	37,000
9	Jewell Enterprises	19,764	50,801	70,565
10				
11				
12				
13				
14				
15				
16				
17				
18				
19				
20				
21				
22				
23				

Sales 2020 | Sales 2021

Figure 5.3 Visual Benchmark - Sales 2021 Worksheet

	A	B	C	D
1	**Clearline Manufacturing**			
2	SEMIANNUAL SALES - 2021			
3	Customer	1st Half	2nd Half	Total
4	Lakeside Trucking	$ 84,300	$ 73,500	$ 157,800
5	Gresham Machines	33,000	40,500	73,500
6	Real Photography	20,750	15,790	36,540
7	Genesis Productions	51,270	68,195	119,465
8	Landower Company	22,000	15,000	37,000
9	Jewell Enterprises	14,470	33,770	48,240
10				
11				
12				
13				
14				
15				
16				
17				
18				
19				
20				
21				
22				
23				

Sales 2020 | Sales 2021

Case Study

Part 1

In your position as an administrator for Gateway Global, an electronics manufacturing corporation, you are gathering information on supplies and equipment expenses. You have gathered information for the first quarter of the year and decide to create a workbook containing worksheets for monthly information. To do this, create a worksheet that contains the following information:

- The company name is *Gateway Global*.
- Create the title *January Expenditures*.
- Create the columns shown in Figure 5.4.
- Insert a formula in the *Total* column that sums the supplies and equipment amounts in each row and insert a formula in the *Total* row that sums the amounts in the *Supplies*, *Equipment*, and *Total* columns.
- Apply formatting such as fill color, borders, font color, font size, and shading to enhance the appearance of the worksheet.

Figure 5.4 Case Study Part 1

Department	Supplies	Equipment	Total
Production	$25,425	$135,500	
Technical Support	14,500	65,000	
Finance	5,790	22,000	
Sales and Marketing	35,425	8,525	
Facilities	6,000	1,200	
Total			

After creating and formatting the worksheet, complete the following:

- Insert a new worksheet and then copy the data in Sheet1 to Sheet2.
- Insert a new worksheet and then copy the data in Sheet1 to Sheet3.
- Make the following changes to the data in Sheet2:
  - Change *January Expenditures* to *February Expenditures*.
  - Change the Production Department supplies amount to *$38,550* and the equipment amount to *$88,500*.
  - Change the Technical Support Department equipment amount to *$44,250*.
  - Change the Finance Department supplies amount to *$7,500*.
- Make the following changes to the data in Sheet3:
  - Change *January Expenditures* to *March Expenditures*.
  - Change the Production Department supplies amount to *$65,000* and the equipment amount to *$150,000*.
  - Change the Technical Support Department supplies amount to *$21,750* and the equipment amount to *$43,525*.
  - Change the Facilities Department equipment amount to *$18,450*.

Create a new worksheet that summarizes the supplies and equipment amounts for January, February, and March. Apply the same formatting to the worksheet as you applied to the other three worksheets. Change the tab name for Sheet1 to *Jan Exps*, the tab name for Sheet2 to *Feb Exps*, the tab name for Sheet3 to *Mar Exps*, and the tab name for Sheet4 to *Qtr Summary*. Change the color of each tab. (You determine the colors.)

Insert a header that prints your name at the left side of each worksheet and the current date at the right side of each worksheet. Save the workbook and name it **5-GGExp**. Print all the worksheets in the workbook and then close the workbook.

Part 2

Employees of Gateway Global have formed two intramural co-ed softball teams and you have volunteered to keep statistics for the players. Open **GGStats** and then make the following changes to both worksheets in the workbook:

- Insert a formula that calculates a player's batting average: Hits / At Bats.
- Insert a formula that calculates a player's on-base percentage: (Walks + Hits) / (At Bats + Walks). Select the range E5:F13 and then specify three digits after the decimal point.
- Insert the company name.
- Apply formatting to enhance the appearance of the worksheets.
- Center the worksheets horizontally and vertically on the page.
- Insert a footer on each worksheet that prints your name at the left and the date at the right.

Use the Help or Tell Me feature to learn about applying cell styles, or click the Cell Styles button in the Styles group on the Home tab and then experiment with applying different styles. Apply the Good cell style to any cell in the *Batting Average* column with a value over 0.400. Apply this style to cells in both worksheets. Save the workbook and name it **5-GGStats**. Print both worksheets and then close **5-GGStats**.

Part 3

Many of the suppliers for Gateway Global are international and use metric measurements. The purchasing manager has asked you to prepare a worksheet in Excel that converts length measurements. Use the internet to locate information on converting the following length measurements:

- 1 inch to centimeters
- 1 foot to meters
- 1 yard to meters
- 1 mile to kilometers

Locate a site on the internet that provides the formula for converting Fahrenheit temperatures to Celsius temperatures and then create another worksheet in the workbook with the following information:

- Insert Fahrenheit temperatures beginning with 0 and continuing to 100 in increments of 5 (for example, 0, 5, 10, 15, and so on).
- Insert a formula that converts each Fahrenheit temperature to a Celsius temperature.

Include the company name, *Gateway Global*, in both worksheets. Apply additional formatting to improve the appearance of the worksheets. Rename each worksheet and apply a color to each tab. (You determine the names and colors.) Save the workbook and name it **5-GGConv**. Print both worksheets centered horizontally and vertically on the page and then close **5-GGConv**.

Part 4

Open Microsoft Word and then create a letterhead document that contains the company name, *Gateway Global*; the address (you decide the street address, city, state, and zip code or street address, city, province, and postal code); and the telephone number (you decide). Apply formatting to improve the appearance of the letterhead. Save the document and name it **5-GGLtrhd**. Save the document again and name it **5-GGConvLtr**.

In Excel, open **5-GGConv** (the workbook you created in Part 3). In the Fahrenheit conversion worksheet, copy the cells containing data and then paste them in **5-GGConvLtr** as a picture object. Center the picture object between the left and right margins. Save, print, and then close **5-GGConvLtr**. Close Microsoft Word and then in Excel close **5-GGConv**.

Maintaining Workbooks

 The online course includes additional review and assessment resources.

Skills Assessment

Assessment
1

Define and Apply Cell Styles to a Projected Earnings Workbook

1. At a blank worksheet, define a style named *C6Heading* that contains the following formatting:
   a. Font: 14-point Cambria bold in standard dark blue
   b. Horizontal alignment: Center alignment
   c. Borders: Top and bottom in standard dark blue (use the thick line style in the second column, fifth row of the *Style* option box)
   d. Fill: Light yellow (eighth column, second row)
2. Define a style named *C6Subheading* that contains the following formatting:
   a. Font: 12-point Cambria bold in standard dark blue
   b. Horizontal alignment: Center alignment
   c. Borders: Top and bottom in standard dark blue (use the thick line style in the second column, fifth row of the *Style* option box)
   d. Fill: Light green (last column, second row)
3. Define a style named *C6Column* that contains the following formatting:
   a. Number: At the Style dialog box, click the *Number* check box to remove the check mark.
   b. Font: 12-point Cambria in standard dark blue
   c. Fill: Light green (last column, second row)
4. Save the workbook and name it **6-Styles**.
5. With **6-Styles** open, open ProjEarnings.
6. Save the workbook and name it **6-ProjEarnings**.
7. Make cell C6 active and then insert a formula that multiplies the percentage in cell B6 by the amount in cell B3. (When writing the formula, identify cell B3 as an absolute reference.) Copy the formula to the range C7:C17.
8. Make cell C6 active and then click the Accounting Number Format button.
9. Copy the styles from **6-Styles** into **6-ProjEarnings**. *Hint: Do this at the Merge Styles dialog box.*
10. Apply the following styles:
    a. Select cells A1 and A2 and then apply the C6Heading style.
    b. Select the range A5:C5 and then apply the C6Subheading style.
    c. Select the range A6:A17 and then apply the C6Column style.
11. Save the workbook and then print **6-ProjEarnings**.

12. With **6-ProjEarnings** open, modify the following styles:
   a. Modify the C6Heading style so it changes the font color to dark green (last column, sixth row), changes the vertical alignment to center alignment, and changes the color of the top and bottom borders to dark green (last column, sixth row).
   b. Modify the C6Subheading style so it changes the font color to dark green (last column, sixth row) and changes the color of the top and bottom borders to dark green (last column, sixth row).
   c. Modify the C6Column style so it changes the font color to dark green (last column, sixth row). Do not change any of the other formatting attributes.
13. Save and then print the workbook.
14. Close **6-ProjEarnings** and then close **6-Styles** without saving the changes.

Assessment 2 — Insert Hyperlinks in a Bookstore Workbook

1. Open **BGSpecials** and then save it with the name **6-BGSpecials**.
2. Make cell E3 active and then create a hyperlink to www.microsoft.com.
3. Make cell E4 active and then create a hyperlink to www.symantec.com.
4. Make cell E5 active and then create a hyperlink to www.nasa.gov.
5. Make cell E6 active and then create a hyperlink to www.cnn.com.
6. Make cell A8 active, type Weekly specials!, and then create a hyperlink to the workbook named **BGWklySpcls**.
7. Click the hyperlink to the Microsoft website, explore the site, and then close the web browser.
8. Click the hyperlink to the NASA website, explore the site, and then close the web browser.
9. Click the Weekly specials! hyperlink, view the workbook, and then close the workbook.
10. Save, print, and then close **6-BGSpecials**.

Assessment 3 — Write a Formula with the PMT Function

1. Open **CMIRefiPlan** and then save it with the name **7-CMIRefiPlan**.
2. The manager of Clearline Manufacturing is interested in refinancing a loan for either $125,000 or $300,000 and wants to determine the monthly payments. Make cell E4 active and then insert a formula using the PMT function. (For assistance, refer to Activity 5a.) The monthly payment amounts will display as negative numbers, representing an outflow of cash.
3. Copy the formula in cell E4 down into the range E5:E7.
4. Save, print, and then close **7-CMRefiPlan**.

Assessment 4 — Write a Formula with the FV Function and Insert Comments

1. Open **CMInvest** and then save it with the name **6-CMInvest**.
2. Make cell B6 active and then use the FV function to insert a formula that calculates the future value of the investment. (For assistance, refer to Activity 5b.)
3. Save and then print the worksheet.
4. Make the following changes to the worksheet:
   a. Change the percentage in cell B3 from *6.5%* to *8.0%*.
   b. Change the number in cell B4 from *48* to *60*.
5. Insert a new comment in cell B3, type The rate needs to be divided by 12 because it is a yearly rate., and then post the comment.
6. Delete the comment in cell B6.

7. Change the print settings so comments print at the end of the sheet.
8. Save, print, and then close **6-CMInvest**.

Assessment 5 Apply Conditional Formatting to a Sales Workbook

1. Use Excel Help files or experiment with the options at the Conditional Formatting button drop-down gallery (in the Styles group on the Home tab) to learn about conditional formatting.
2. Open **PSSales** and then save it with the name **6-PSSales**.
3. Select the range D5:D19 and then use conditional formatting to display the amounts as data bars. (You choose the type of data bars.)
4. Insert a header that prints your name, a page number, and the current date.
5. Save, print, and then close **6-PSSales**.

Visual Benchmark

Fill in an Expense Report Form

1. Display the New backstage area, search for an expense report template, and then double-click the *Expense report* template shown in Figure 6.1. (If this template is not available for download, open **ExpenseReport** from your EL1C6 folder.)
2. Apply the Note cell style to the cells K1 and L1.
3. Type the information in the cells as shown in Figure 6.1.
4. Make cell L15 active and then apply the Good cell style.
5. Select the range L14:L16 and then apply the Accounting format.
6. Delete any empty expense rows in the report.
7. Save the completed workbook and name it **6-OEExpRpt**.
8. Print and then close **6-OEExpRpt**.

Figure 6.1 Visual Benchmark

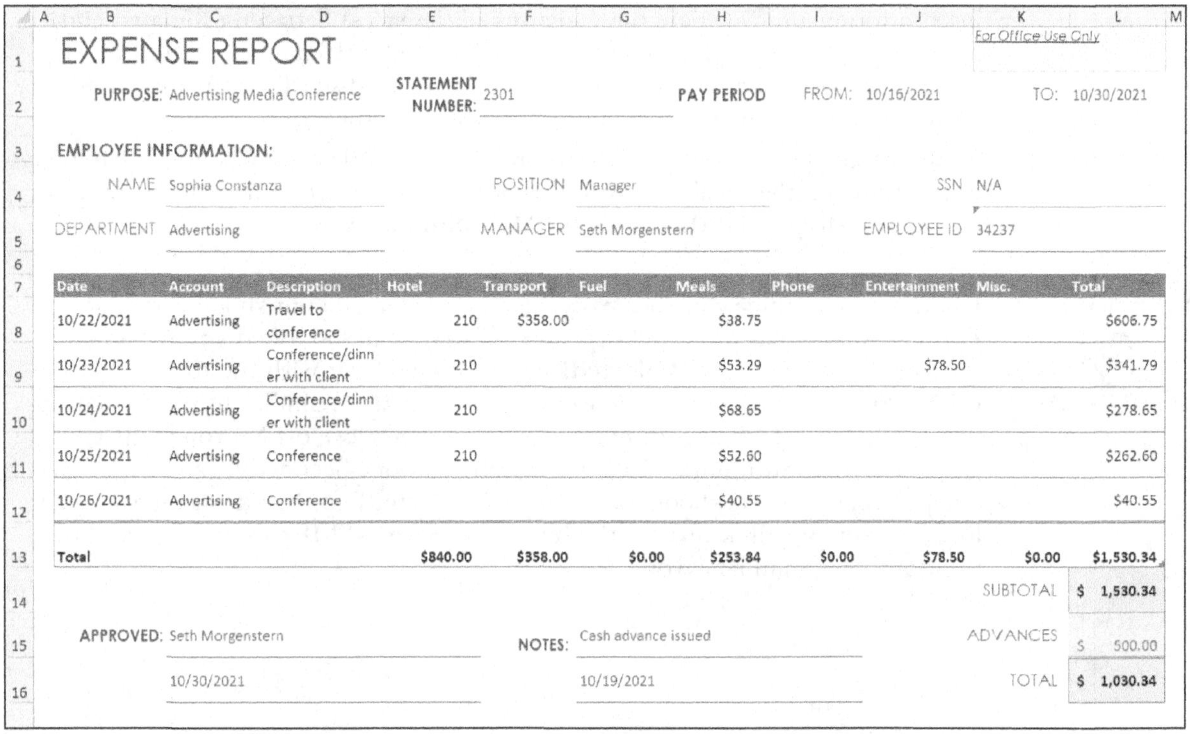

EXPENSE REPORT

For Office Use Only

PURPOSE: Advertising Media Conference | STATEMENT NUMBER: 2301 | PAY PERIOD FROM: 10/16/2021 TO: 10/30/2021

EMPLOYEE INFORMATION:

NAME Sophia Constanza | POSITION Manager | SSN N/A

DEPARTMENT Advertising | MANAGER Seth Morgenstern | EMPLOYEE ID 34237

Date	Account	Description	Hotel	Transport	Fuel	Meals	Phone	Entertainment	Misc.	Total
10/22/2021	Advertising	Travel to conference	210	$358.00		$38.75				$606.75
10/23/2021	Advertising	Conference/dinner with client	210			$53.29		$78.50		$341.79
10/24/2021	Advertising	Conference/dinner with client	210			$68.65				$278.65
10/25/2021	Advertising	Conference	210			$52.60				$262.60
10/26/2021	Advertising	Conference				$40.55				$40.55
Total			$840.00	$358.00	$0.00	$253.84	$0.00	$78.50	$0.00	$1,530.34

SUBTOTAL $ 1,530.34

APPROVED: Seth Morgenstern 10/30/2021 | NOTES: Cash advance issued 10/19/2021 | ADVANCES $ 500.00

TOTAL $ 1,030.34

Case Study

You are the office manager for Leeward Marine and decide to consolidate into one workbook several worksheets containing information on expenses. Open **LMEstExp** and then save it with the name **6-LMExpSummary**. Open **LMActExp**, copy the worksheet into **6-LMExpSummary** after Sheet1, make **LMActExp** the active workbook, and then close it. Apply appropriate formatting to the numbers and insert the necessary formulas in each worksheet. (Use the Clear button on the Home tab to clear the contents of cells N8, N9, N13, and N14 in both worksheets.) Include the company name in both worksheets. Create styles and apply them to the cells in both worksheets to maintain consistent formatting. Automatically adjust the widths of the columns to accommodate the longest entries. Save **6-LMExpSummary**.

As the office manager for Leeward Marine, you decide to include in the workbook another worksheet that displays the yearly estimated expenses, actual expenses, and variances (differences) between the two. With **6-LMExpSummary** open, open **LMExpVar**. Copy the worksheet into **6-LMExpSummary** as the last worksheet, make **LMExpVar** the active workbook, and then close it. Rename the sheet tab containing estimated expenses as *Estimated Exp*, rename the sheet tab containing actual expenses as *Actual Exp*, and rename the sheet tab containing variances as *Summary*. Apply a different color to each of the three sheet tabs you just renamed.

Select the yearly estimated expense amounts (column N) in the Estimated Exp worksheet and then paste them in the appropriate cells in the Summary worksheet. Click the Paste Options button and then click the Values & Number Formatting button in the *Paste Values* section of the drop-down list. (This pastes the value and the cell formatting, rather than just the formula.) Select the yearly actual expense amounts (column N) in the Actual Exp worksheet and then paste them in the appropriate cells in the Summary worksheet. Click the Paste Options button and then click the Values & Number Formatting button in the *Paste Values* section of the drop-down list. Apply appropriate formatting to the numbers and insert a formula to calculate the variances (differences) between estimated and actual expenses. Clear the contents of cells D8, D9, D13, and D14. Add the company name and apply styles to the Summary worksheet so it is formatted similarly to the Estimated Exp and Actual Exp worksheets.

Insert an appropriate header or footer in each worksheet. Change to landscape orientation and then scale the worksheets so each prints on one page. Save, print all the worksheets, and then close **6-LMExpSummary**.

Based on the summary of the yearly expense variances, your supervisor at Leeward Marine has projected expenses for next year and asked you to format the worksheet. Open **LMProjectedExp** and then save it with the name **6-LMProjectedExp**. Format the worksheet in a manner similar to the formatting you applied to **6-LMExpSummary**. Save and then close **6-LMProjectedExp**. Open **6-LMExpSummary**, make the Summary worksheet active, and then insert a hyperlink to the workbook named **6-LMProjectedExp**. You determine the cell location and hyperlink text for the hyperlink. Save **6-LMExpSummary** and then print only the Summary worksheet.

Part 4

You need to print a number of copies of the summary worksheet in **6-LMExpSummary** and you want the Leeward Marine letterhead to print at the tops of the pages. You decide to use the letterhead in a Word document and copy the summary data from Excel into the Word document. To do this, open Word and then open the document **LMLtrhd** from your EL1C6 folder. Press the Enter key two times. Make Excel the active program and with **6-LMExpSummary** open, make the Summary worksheet active, select and then copy the cells containing information on the yearly expense variances (include the subtitle and all columns but not the hyperlink), and then paste them into the **LMLtrhd** document as a picture object. (Click the Paste Options button and then click the Picture button.) Save the document with the name **6-LMExpSumDoc**. Print and then close **6-LMExpSumDoc** and then close Word. In Excel, close **6-LMExpSummary**.

Creating Charts and Inserting Formulas

 The online course includes additional review and assessment resources.

Skills Assessment

Assessment 1

Create a Net Profit Chart

1. Open **NetProfit** and then save it with the name **7-NetProfit**.
2. Select the range A2:E7 and then create a chart using the Recommended Charts button. (Accept the chart recommended by Excel.)
3. Use the Chart Elements button outside the right border of the chart to insert a data table and remove the legend.
4. Use the Chart Styles button outside the right border of the chart to apply the Style 7 chart style.
5. Use the Chart Filters button outside the right border of the chart to display only the New York and Philadelphia net profits in the chart. (Make sure you click the Apply button.)
6. Click in the *Chart Title* placeholder text, type Net Profit by Office, and then press the Enter key.
7. Move the chart below the cells containing data, deselect the chart, make sure the data and chart fit on one page, and then print the worksheet (data and chart).
8. Save and then close **7-NetProfit**.

Assessment 2

Create a Company Sales Column Chart

1. Open **CMSales** and then save it with the name **7-CMSales**.
2. Select the range A3:C15 and then create a column chart with the following specifications:
   a. Click the *3-D Clustered Column* option at the Insert Column or Bar Chart button drop-down gallery.
   b. Click the Quick Layout button in the Chart Layouts group on the Chart Tools Design tab and then click the *Layout 3* option (third column, first row at the drop-down gallery) at the drop-down gallery.
   c. Apply the Style 11 chart style.
   d. Click in the *Chart Title* placeholder text, type 2021 Company Sales, and then press the Enter key.
   e. Move the chart to a new sheet.
3. Print only the worksheet containing the chart.
4. Save and then close **7-CMSales**.

Assessment

3

Create Quarterly Domestic and Foreign Sales Bar Chart

1. Open **CMPQtrlySales** and then save it with the name **7-CMPQtrlySales**.
2. Select the range A3:E5 and then create a bar chart with the following specifications:
   a. Click the *3-D Clustered Bar* option at the Insert Column or Bar Chart button drop-down gallery.
   b. Use the Quick Layout button to apply the Layout 2 quick layout (second column, first row at the drop-down gallery).
   c. Apply the Style 6 chart style.
   d. Type Quarterly Sales as the chart title. (Excel will convert the text to uppercase letters.)
   e. Click in the chart but outside any chart element.
   f. Click the Chart Tools Format tab and then apply the Subtle Effect - Gold, Accent 4 shape style (fifth column, fourth row).
   g. Click the Chart Elements button arrow, click *Series "Foreign"* at the drop-down list, and then apply the standard dark red shape fill. (Use the Shape Fill button arrow in the Shape Styles group and click *Dark Red* in the *Standard Colors* section.)
   h. Select the chart title and then apply the Fill - Black, Text 1, Shadow WordArt style (first column, first row).
   i. Increase the height of the chart to 4 inches and the width to 6 inches.
3. Move the chart below the cells containing data, deselect the chart, make sure the data and chart fit on one page, and then print the worksheet (data and chart).
4. Save and then close **7-CMPQtrlySales**.

Assessment

4

Create a Fund Allocations Pie Chart

1. Open **SMFFunds** and then save it with the name **7-SMFFunds**.
2. Select the range A3:B7 and then create a pie chart with the following specifications:
   a. Click the *3-D Pie* option at the Insert Pie or Doughnut Chart button drop-down gallery.
   b. Apply the Layout 1 quick layout (first column, first row at the drop-down gallery).
   c. Apply the Style 2 chart style.
   d. Change the color to Colorful Palette 3.
   e. Move the pie chart to a new worksheet.
   f. Change the title to *Fund Allocations*.
   g. Click the Chart Tools Format tab, make sure the chart (not a chart element) is selected, and then click the Format Selection button.
   h. At the Format Chart Area task pane, make sure the Fill & Line icon is active, click *Fill* to display additional fill options, click the *Gradient fill* option, and then close the task pane.
   i. Use the *Chart Elements* option box arrow to select *Series "Allocation" Data Labels*.
   j. With the data labels selected, click the Text Fill button arrow (in the WordArt Styles group) and then click the *Orange, Accent 2, Darker 50%* option (sixth column, bottom row in the *Theme Colors* section).
   k. With the data labels still selected, click the Home tab and then change the font size to 18 points.
3. Print only the worksheet containing the chart.
4. Save and then close **7-SMFFunds**.

Assessment 5   Write a Formula with the IF Function

1. Open **DISalesBonuses** and then save it with the name **7-DISalesBonuses**.
2. Insert a formula in cell C4 that inserts the word *YES* if the amount in B4 is greater than 99999 and *NO* if the amount is not greater than 99999. Copy the formula in cell C4 to the range C5:C14.
3. Make cell D4 active and then type the formula =IF(C4="YES",B4*0.05,0). If sales are over $99,999, this formula will multiply the sales amount by 5% and then insert the product (result) of the formula in the cell. Copy the formula in cell D4 to the range D5:D14.
4. Apply to cell D4 the Accounting format with a dollar symbol and no digits after the decimal point.
5. Save and then print **7-DISalesBonuses**.
6. Display the formulas in the worksheet and then print it.
7. Turn off the display of formulas.
8. Save and then close **7-DISalesBonuses**.

Assessment 6   Create a Stacked Column Chart

1. Use Excel's Help feature to learn more about chart types and specifically stacked column charts.
2. Open **CMPerSales** and then save it with the name **7-CMPerSales**.
3. With the data in the worksheet, create a three-dimensional 100% stacked column chart in a separate sheet. Create an appropriate title for the chart and apply other formatting to enhance the appearance of the chart.
4. Print only the worksheet containing the chart.
5. Close **7-CMPerSales**.

Assessment 7   Learn about Excel Options

1. Learn about specific options in the Excel Options dialog box by completing the following steps:
   a. At a blank workbook, display the Excel Options dialog box by clicking the File tab and then clicking *Options*.
   b. At the Excel Options dialog box, click the *Advanced* option in the left panel.
   c. Scroll down the dialog box and look for the section *Display options for this workbook* and then read the information. Also read the information in the *Display options for this worksheet* section.
   d. Write down the check box options available in the *Display options for this workbook* section and the *Display options for this worksheet* section and identify whether each check box contains a check mark. (Record only check box options and ignore buttons and options preceded by circles.)
2. With the information you wrote down about the options, create an Excel worksheet with the following information:
   a. In column C, type each option you wrote down. (Include an appropriate column heading.)
   b. In column B, insert an *X* in each cell that precedes an option with a check mark in the check box. (Include an appropriate column heading.)
   c. In column A, write a formula with the IF function that inserts the word *ON* in the cell if the cell in column B contains an *X* and *OFF* if it does not (the cell is blank). (Include an appropriate column heading.)
   d. Apply formatting to enhance the appearance of the worksheet.

3. Save the workbook and name it **7-DisplayOptions**.
4. Turn on the display of formulas.
5. Print the worksheet.
6. Turn off the display of formulas.
7. Save, print, and then close **7-DisplayOptions**.

Visual Benchmark

Create and Format a Pie Chart

1. At a blank workbook, enter data and then create a pie chart in a separate sheet, as shown in Figure 7.1. Use the information shown in the pie chart to create the data. (To match the pie chart in the figure, type the expenses in this order: Supplies, Utilities, Advertising, Marketing, Lease, Taxes, and then Salaries.) Format the pie chart so it appears similarly to the one in Figure 7.1. (Apply the Layout 4 quick style and the Style 8 chart style. Create and format the title as shown in the figure and change the size of the data labels to 12 points.)
2. Save the completed workbook and name it **7-CMFebExp**.
3. Print both worksheets in the workbook.
4. Close **7-CMFebExp**.

Figure 7.1 Visual Benchmark

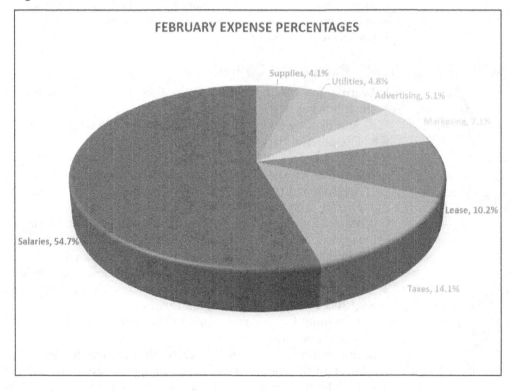

Case Study

You are an administrator for Dollar Wise Financial Services and need to prepare a chart that represents the amounts of home loans and commercial loans for the past year. Use the information below to prepare a chart in Excel. You determine the type and style of the chart and the layout and formatting. Insert a shape in the chart that contains the text *All-time High* and points to the Commercial Loans series second-quarter amount (*$6,785,250*).

Home Loans

1st Qtr.	=	$2,675,025
2nd Qtr.	=	$3,125,750
3rd Qtr.	=	$1,975,425
4th Qtr.	=	$875,650

Commercial Loans

1st Qtr.	=	$5,750,980
2nd Qtr.	=	$6,785,250
3rd Qtr.	=	$4,890,625
4th Qtr.	=	$2,975,900

Save the workbook and name it **7-DWQtrSales**. Print only the chart and then close **7-DWQtrSales**.

Your supervisor at Dollar Wise Financial Services has asked you to present information on the company's budget. You have the dollar amounts and need to convert each amount to a percentage of the entire budget. Use the information below to calculate the percentage of the budget for each item and then create a pie chart using the information. *Hint: The formula will divide the amount of a budget item by the total budget amount.* You determine the chart style, layout, and formatting.

Total Budget: $6,000,000

Building Costs	=	$720,000
Salaries	=	$2,340,000
Benefits	=	$480,000
Advertising	=	$840,000
Marketing	=	$600,000
Client Expenses	=	$480,000
Equipment	=	$420,000
Supplies	=	$120,000

Save the workbook containing the pie chart and name it **7-DWBudget**. Print only the chart and then close **7-DWBudget**.

The loan officer for Dollar Wise Financial Services has asked you to prepare a sample home mortgage worksheet to show prospective clients. This mortgage worksheet will show the monthly payments on differently priced homes with varying down payments. Open the worksheet named **DWMortgagesWksht** and then complete the home mortgage worksheet by inserting the following formulas:

- Since many homes in your area sell for at least $400,000, you decide to use that amount in the worksheet with down payments of 5%, 10%, 15%, and 20%. (Insert the amount *$400,000* to the range A11:A14.)
- In column C, insert a formula that determines the down payment amount.
- In column D, insert a formula that determines the loan amount.

- In column G, insert a formula using the PMT function. (The monthly payment will display as a negative number.)
- Use the fill handle to fill all the formulas into row 14.

Save the worksheet and name it **7-DWMortgagesWksht**.

Part 4

You know from working with the loan officer at Dollar Wise Financial Services that if a home buyer puts down less than 20% of the home's purchase price, he or she is required to have mortgage insurance. With **7-DWMortgagesWksht** open, insert an IF statement in the cells in column H that inserts the word *NO* if the percentage in column B is equal to or greater than 20% and inserts the word *YES* if the percentage in column B is less than 20%. Save and then print **7-DWMortgagesWksht**.

Part 5

The loan officer at Dollar Wise Financial Services has asked you to prepare information on mortgage interest rates for a community presentation. You decide to provide the information in a chart for easy viewing. Use the internet to search for historical data on the national average for mortgage interest rates. Determine the average mortgage rate for a 30-year FRM (fixed-rate mortgage) for each January and July beginning with the year 2016 and continuing to the current year. Use this information to create the chart. Save the workbook and name it **7-DWRates**. Print only the chart and then close **7-DWRates**.

Adding Visual Interest to Workbooks

 The online course includes additional review and assessment resources.

Skills Assessment

Assessment 1

Insert an Image and WordArt in an Equipment Sales Workbook

1. Open **MSSalesPlans** and then save it with the name **8-MSSalesPlans**.
2. Insert a formula in cell E4 using the PMT function that calculates monthly payments. (Type a minus symbol [–] before the cell designation in the *Pv* text box at the Function Arguments dialog box.) ***Hint: For assistance, refer to Chapter 6, Activity 5a.***
3. Copy the formula in cell E4 into cells E5 and E6.
4. Insert a formula in cell F4 that calculates the total amount of the payments.
5. Copy the formula in cell F4 into cells F5 and F6.
6. Insert a formula in cell G4 that calculates the total amount of interest paid.
7. Copy the formula in cell G4 into cells G5 and G6.
8. Insert the image shown in Figure 8.1 with the following specifications:
   a. Click the Insert tab and then click the Pictures button.
   b. At the Insert Picture dialog box, navigate to your EL1C8 folder and then double-click the image file *MapleLeaf*.
   c. Apply the Orange, Accent color 2 Dark color (third column, second row in the *Recolor* section).
   d. Apply the Brightness: 0% Contrast: -20% correction (third column, second row in the *Brightness/Contrast* section).
   e. Apply the Drop Shadow Rectangle picture style (fourth option in the Picture Styles gallery).
   f. Size and move the image so it is positioned as shown in Figure 8.1.
9. Insert the company name *Maplewood Suppliers* in cell A1 as WordArt with the following specifications:
   a. Click the WordArt button on the Insert tab and then click the option in the fourth column, third row (orange outline with white fill).
   b. Apply the Orange, Accent 2, Darker 50% text fill (sixth column, last row in the *Theme Colors* section).
   c. Apply the Orange, Accent 2, Lighter 60% text outline (sixth column, third row in the *Theme Colors* section).
   d. Using the Text Effects button, apply the Square transform text effect (first option in the *Warp* section).
   e. Change the width of the WordArt to 5 inches.
   f. Move the WordArt so it is positioned in cell A1, as shown in Figure 8.1.
10. Change to landscape orientation.
11. Save, print, and then close **8-MSSalesPlans**.

Figure 8.1 Assessment 1

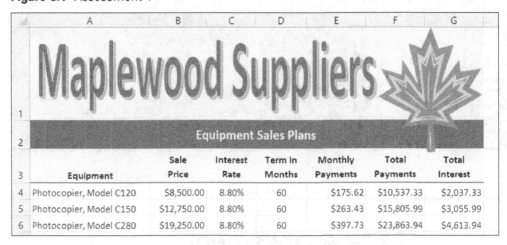

Equipment	Sale Price	Interest Rate	Term in Months	Monthly Payments	Total Payments	Total Interest
Photocopier, Model C120	$8,500.00	8.80%	60	$175.62	$10,537.33	$2,037.33
Photocopier, Model C150	$12,750.00	8.80%	60	$263.43	$15,805.99	$3,055.99
Photocopier, Model C280	$19,250.00	8.80%	60	$397.73	$23,863.94	$4,613.94

Assessment 2

Insert Formulas and an Icon and Format a Travel Company Workbook

1. Open **TSGEVacs** and then save it with the name **8-TSGEVacs**.
2. Insert appropriate formulas to calculate the prices based on 10% and 20% discounts and then apply the appropriate number formatting. *Hint: For the 10% discount column, multiply the price per person by 0.90 (which determines 90% of the price) and for the 20% discount column, multiply the price per person by 0.80 (which determines 80% of the price).*
3. Format the image of the airplane and position it as shown in Figure 8.2 with the following specifications:
   a. Remove some of the background from the image. (To do this, click the Remove Background button in the Adjust group on the Picture Tools Format tab. Click the Mark Areas to Keep button, click around the sun image until it displays similar to what is shown in Figure 8.2, and then click the Keep Changes button.)
   b. Rotate the image to flip it horizontally.
   c. Apply the Brightness: +20% Contrast: +20% correction (fourth column, fourth row in the *Brightness/Contrast* section).
   d. Change the height of the image to 1.4 inches and then position the image as shown in the figure.
4. Open Word and then open **TSAirfare** from your EL1C8 folder. Click the Excel button on the taskbar and then use the Screenshot button (with the *Screen Clipping* option) to select and then insert the airfare information in **8-TSGEVacs**. Position the information at the right of the data in the worksheet.
5. Change to landscape orientation.
6. Insert and format the map compass icon as shown in Figure 8.2 with the following specifications:
   a. Display the Insert Icons window, click the *Location* category, click the map compass icon, and then click the Insert button.
   b. Apply the Colored Fill - Accent 1, Dark 1 Outline graphic style (second column, third row at the drop-down gallery).
   c. Change the size of the icon and then position the image as shown in the figure.
7. Make sure the data and the airfare information display on one page and then print the worksheet.
8. Save and then close **8-TSGEVacs**.

Figure 8.2 Assessment 2

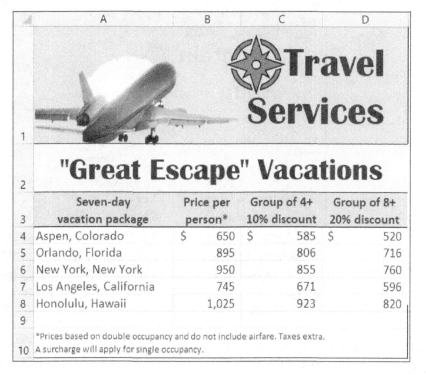

	Seven-day vacation package	Price per person*	Group of 4+ 10% discount	Group of 8+ 20% discount
4	Aspen, Colorado	$ 650	$ 585	$ 520
5	Orlando, Florida	895	806	716
6	New York, New York	950	855	760
7	Los Angeles, California	745	671	596
8	Honolulu, Hawaii	1,025	923	820

*Prices based on double occupancy and do not include airfare. Taxes extra.
A surcharge will apply for single occupancy.

9. Click the Word button on the taskbar, close **TSAirfare**, and then close Word.

Assessment 3

Insert and Format Shapes in a Company Sales Workbook

1. Open **MGSales** and then save it with the name **8-MGSales**.
2. Use the Isosceles Triangle shape in the *Basic Shapes* section of the Shapes drop-down palette to draw a triangle, as shown in Figure 8.3.
3. Apply Green, Accent 6, Darker 50% shape outline color (last column, last row in the *Theme Colors* section) to the triangle.
4. Apply Green, Accent 6, Darker 25% shape fill (last column, fifth row in the *Theme Colors* section) to the triangle.
5. Copy the triangle three times.
6. Position and arrange the triangles as shown in Figure 8.3. (Use the Send Backward button on the Drawing Tools Format tab for the first and third triangles to move them behind the other triangles.)
7. Select the second and fourth triangles and then apply the Green, Accent 6, Lighter 80% shape fill (last column, second row in the *Theme Colors* section).
8. Insert the total amounts in the range B10:D10.
9. Insert an arrow pointing to *$97,549* with the following specifications:
   a. Use the Left Arrow shape to draw the arrow.
   b. Change the height of the arrow to 0.6 inch and the width to 1.2 inches.
   c. Apply Green, Accent 6, Darker 25% shape fill and shape outline (last column, fifth row in the *Theme Colors* section) to the arrow.
   d. Type the text Largest Order in the arrow and then select the text. Change the font to Candara, change the font size to 10 points, and apply bold formatting.
   e. Position the arrow as shown in Figure 8.3.
10. Format the worksheet as shown in Figure 8.3.
11. Save, print, and then close **8-MGSales**.

Figure 8.3 Assessment 3

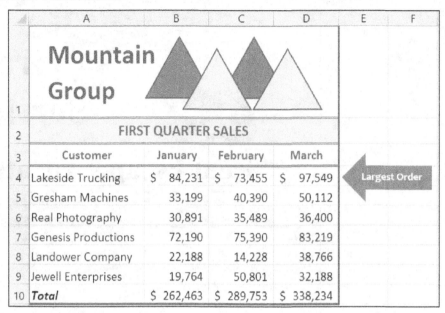

Insert and Format a SmartArt Graphic in a Sales Workbook

Assessment

4

1. Open **PS2ndQtrSales** and then save it with the name **8-PS2ndQtrSales**.
2. Change to landscape orientation.
3. Insert the Pyramid List SmartArt graphic at the right of the worksheet data with the following specifications:
   a. Apply the Gradient Loop - Accent 2 color (fourth option in the *Accent 2* section).
   b. Apply the Cartoon SmartArt style (third column, first row in the *3-D* section).
   c. In the bottom text box, type Red Level, press the Enter key, and then type $25,000 to $49,999.
   d. In the middle text box, type Blue Level, press the Enter key, and then type $50,000 to $99,999.
   e. In the top text box, type Gold Level, press the Enter key, and then type $100,000+.
   f. Apply fill color to each text box to match the level color. (Use the Orange fill color for the *Gold Level* text box.)
4. Size and/or move the SmartArt graphic so it displays attractively at the right of the worksheet data. (Make sure the entire graphic will print on the same page as the worksheet data.)
5. Save, print, and then close **8-PS2ndQtrSales**.

Insert and Modify a 3D Model

Assessment

5

1. Open **RPRefiPlan** and then save it with the name **8-RPRefiPlan**.
2. Insert a formula in cell E4 using the PMT function that calculates monthly payments. (Type a minus symbol [–] before the cell designation in the *Pv* text box at the Function Arguments dialog box.) Copy the formula in cell E4 into the range E5:E7 without formatting.
3. Insert a formula in cell F4 that calculates the total amount paid during the duration of the loan, including interest, by multiplying the contents of cells D4 and E4. Copy the formula in cell F4 into the range F5:F7 without formatting.

4. Insert the camera 3D model shown in Figure 8.4 with the following specifications:
   a. Display the Online 3D Models window.
   b. Click the *Electronics and Gadgets* category.
   c. Insert the model of the camera shown in Figure 8.4.
   d. Use the 3D control to rotate and tilt the camera model.
   e. Size and position the camera model as shown in Figure 8.4.
5. Save and then close **8-RPRefiPlan**.

Figure 8.4 Assessment 5

	A	B	C	D	E	F
1						
2			Refinance Plan			
3	Lender	Amount	Interest Rate	Term in Months	Monthly Payments	Total Paid
4	Castle Credit Union	$ 400,000	6.50%	300	$ 2,700.83	$ 810,248.59
5	Castle Credit Union	500,000	6.20%	300	3,282.91	984,873.14
6	Millstone Bank	400,000	6.40%	240	2,958.79	710,109.64
7	Millstone Bank	500,000	6.10%	240	3,611.06	866,654.48
8						

Visual Benchmark

Insert Formulas, WordArt, an Image, and a Shape in a Worksheet

1. Open **TSYrlySales** and then save it with the name **8-TSYrlySales**.
2. Insert formulas that will calculate the results shown in the worksheet in Figure 8.5. (**Do not** type the data in the cells. Instead, insert the following formulas. The results of your formulas should match the results shown in the figure.)
   - In the range C4:C14, insert a formula with an IF function that inserts *5%* if the amount in the cell in column B is greater than $249,999 and *2%* if the amount is not greater than $249,999. (Note: When creating the formula, omit the comma and dollar sign from the amount 249999.)
   - In the range D4:D14, insert a formula that multiplies the amount in column B with the amount in column C.
   - Apply to cell D4 the Accounting format with a dollar symbol and no digits past the decimal point.
3. Insert the company name *Target Supplies* as WordArt with the following specifications:
   - Choose the *Fill: Black, Text color 1; Outline: White, Background color 1; Hard Shadow: Blue, Accent color 5* option (second column, third row).
   - To type the WordArt text, press Ctrl + L (which applies left text alignment), type Target, press the Enter key, and then type Supplies.

- Apply Orange, Accent 2, Darker 50% text fill color (sixth column, last row in the *Theme Colors* section).
- Apply the Orange, Accent 2, Lighter 40% text outline color (sixth column, fourth row in the *Theme Colors* section).
- Move the WordArt so it is positioned as shown in Figure 8.5.

4. Insert the **Target** image from your EL1C8 folder with the following specifications:
- Apply the Orange, Accent color 2 Light color (third column, third row in the *Recolor* section).
- Apply the Brightness: -40% Contrast: +40% correction (first column, last row in the *Brightness/Contrast* section).
- Size and position the image as shown in the figure.

5. Draw the shape that displays below the data with the following specifications:
- Use the Rectangle: Beveled shape (located in the *Basic Shapes* section).
- Type the text in the shape, apply bold formatting, and then apply center and middle alignment.
- Apply the Orange, Accent 2, Darker 50% shape fill color (sixth column, last row in the *Theme Colors* section).
- Apply the Orange, Accent 2 shape outline color (sixth column, first row in the *Theme Colors* section).

6. Save and then print the worksheet.
7. Turn on the display of formulas and then print the worksheet again.
8. Turn off the display of formulas and then close the workbook.

Figure 8.5 Visual Benchmark

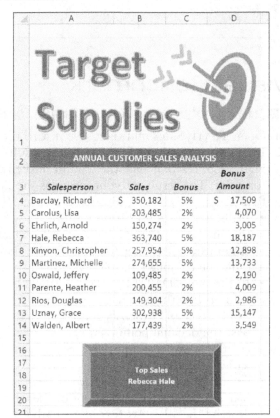

Case Study

Part

1

As the office manager for Ocean Truck Sales, you are responsible for maintaining a spreadsheet of the truck and SUV inventory. Open **OTSales** and then save it with the name **8-OTSales**. Apply formatting to enhance the appearance of the worksheet and insert at least one image (related to a truck or ocean). Save **8-OTSales** and then print the worksheet.

Part

2

With **8-OTSales** open, save it with the name **8-OTSalesF&C**. You make the inventory workbook available to each salesperson at Ocean Truck Sales at the beginning of the week. For easier viewing, divide the workbook into two worksheets, with one worksheet containing all Ford vehicles and the other containing all Chevrolet vehicles. Rename the worksheet tabs to reflect the contents. Sort the data in each worksheet by price from most expensive to least expensive.

The owner of Ocean Truck Sales offers incentives each week to help motivate the salespeople. Insert in the first worksheet a SmartArt graphic of your choosing that contains the following information:

> Small-sized truck: $200
>
> 2WD regular cab: $150
>
> SUV 4x4: $100

Copy the SmartArt graphic in the first worksheet and then paste it into the second worksheet. Change both worksheets to landscape orientation and then save and print both worksheets. Close **8-OTSalesF&C**.

Part

3

Your supervisor at Ocean Truck Sales has asked you to save the inventory worksheet as a web page for viewing online. Open **8-OTSales**, display the Save As dialog box, click the *Save as type* option, and then determine how to save the workbook as a single-file web page. Save the workbook as a single-file web page with the name **8-OTSales-WebPage**. Open your internet browser and then open the web page. Look at the information in the file and then close the internet browser.

Part

4

As part of your weekly duties at Ocean Truck Sales, you post the incentive SmartArt graphic in various locations throughout the company. You decide to insert the graphic in PowerPoint for easy printing. Open **8-OTSalesF&C** and then open PowerPoint. Change the slide layout in PowerPoint to Blank. Copy the SmartArt graphic in the first worksheet and then paste it into the PowerPoint blank slide. Increase and/or move the graphic so it better fills the slide. Print the slide and then close PowerPoint without saving the presentation. Close **8-OTSalesF&C**.

Unit 2 Performance Assessment

 Data Files

Before beginning unit work, copy the EL1U2 folder to your
storage medium and then make EL1U2 the active folder.

Assessing Proficiency

In this unit, you have learned how to work with multiple windows; move, copy,
link, and paste data within and between workbooks and programs; create and
customize charts with data in a worksheet; write formulas with PMT, FV, and
IF functions; save a workbook as a web page; insert hyperlinks; and insert and
customize images, shapes, icons, 3D models, SmartArt graphics, and WordArt.

Assessment 1

Copy and Paste Data and Insert WordArt in a Training Scores Workbook

1. Open **RLTraining** and then save it with the name **U2-RLTraining**.
2. Delete row 15 (the row for *Kwieciak, Kathleen*).
3. Insert a formula in cell D4 that averages the percentages in cells B4
   and C4.
4. Copy the formula in cell D4 down to the range D5:D20.
5. Make cell A22 active, turn on bold formatting, and then type
   Highest Averages.
6. Display the Clipboard task pane and make sure it is empty.
7. Select and then copy each of the following rows (individually): 7, 10, 14, 16,
   and 18.
8. Make cell A23 active and then paste row 14 (the row for *Jewett, Troy*).
9. Make cell A24 active and then paste row 7 (the row for *Cumpston, Kurt*).
10. Make cell A25 active and then paste row 10 (the row for *Fisher-Edwards,
    Theresa*).
11. Make cell A26 active and then paste row 16 (the row for *Mathias, Caleb*).
12. Make cell A27 active and then paste row 18 (the row for *Nyegaard, Curtis*).
13. Click the Clear All button in the Clipboard task pane and then close the task
    pane.
14. Insert in cell A1 the text *Roseland* as WordArt. Format the WordArt text to add
    visual interest to the worksheet.
15. Save, print, and then close **U2-RLTraining**.

Assessment 2

Manage Multiple Worksheets in a Projected Earnings Workbook

1. Open **RLProjEarnings** and then save it with the name **U2-RLProjEarnings**.
2. Delete *Roseland* in cell A1. Open **U2-RLTraining**, copy the *Roseland* WordArt text, and then paste it into cell A1 in **U2-RLProjEarnings**. If necessary, increase the height of row 1 to accommodate the WordArt text.
3. Close **U2-RLTraining**.
4. Insert a new worksheet in the **U2-RLProjEarnings** workbook.
5. Select the range A1:C11 in Sheet1 and then copy and paste the cells to Sheet2, keeping the source column widths.
6. With Sheet2 displayed, make the following changes:
   a. Delete the contents of cell B2.
   b. Change the contents of the following cells:

A6	Change *January* to *July*
A7	Change *February* to *August*
A8	Change *March* to *September*
A9	Change *April* to *October*
A10	Change *May* to *November*
A11	Change *June* to *December*
B6	Change *8.30%* to *8.10%*
B8	Change *9.30%* to *8.70%*

7. Make cell B2 active in Sheet2 and then link to cell B2 in Sheet1.
8. Rename Sheet1 *First Half* and rename Sheet2 *Second Half*.
9. Make the First Half worksheet active and then determine the effect on projected monthly earnings if the projected yearly income is increased by 10% by changing the number in cell B2 to *$1,480,380*.
10. Horizontally and vertically center both worksheets in the workbook and insert a custom header with your name at the left, the current date in the center, and the sheet name at the right (click the Sheet Name button in the Header & Footer Elements group on the Header & Footer Tools Design tab).
11. Save and then print both worksheets.
12. Determine the effect on projected monthly earnings if the projected yearly income is increased by 20% by changing the number in cell B2 to *$1,614,960*.
13. Save the workbook again and then print both worksheets.
14. Close **U2-RLProjEarnings**.

Assessment 3

Create Charts in Worksheets in a Sales Totals Workbook

1. Open **EPYrlySales** and then save it with the name **U2-EPYrlySales**.
2. Rename Sheet1 as *2019 Sales*, rename Sheet2 as *2020 Sales*, and rename Sheet3 as *2021 Sales*.
3. Select all three sheet tabs, make cell A12 active, turn on bold formatting, and then type Total. Make cell B12 active and then insert a formula to total the amounts in the range B4:B11. Make cell C12 active and then insert a formula to total the amounts in the range C4:C11.
4. Make the 2019 Sales worksheet active, select the range A3:C11 (being careful not to select the totals in row 12), and then create a clustered column chart. Click the Switch Row/Column button on the Chart Tools Design tab. Apply formatting to enhance the appearance of the chart. Drag the chart below the worksheet data. (Make sure the chart fits on one page.)

5. Make the 2020 Sales worksheet active and then create the same type of chart you created in Step 4.
6. Make the 2021 Sales worksheet active and then create the same type of chart you created in Step 4. Filter the records in this chart so that only the following companies are shown: *Harbor Manufacturing*, *Avalon Clinic*, and *Stealth Media*.
7. Save the workbook and then print the entire workbook.
8. Close **U2-EPYrlySales**.

Assessment 4

Create a Line Chart and Insert a Comment

1. Open **ProfitCompare** and then save it with the name **U2-ProfitCompare**.
2. Use the data in the workbook to create a line chart with the following specifications:
   a. Apply the Style 11 chart style.
   b. Include the chart title *NET PROFIT COMPARISON*.
   c. Apply the standard green shape fill and shape outline color to the Asia series.
   d. Move the chart below the data.
3. Insert the following new comment in cell E2: *This was the lowest combined sales year*.
4. Set comments to print at the end of the sheet.
5. Save, print, and close **U2-ProfitCompare**.

Assessment 5

Create a Pie Chart and Insert an Icon

1. Open **EPProdDept** and then save it with the name **U2-EPProdDept**.
2. Create a pie chart as a separate worksheet with the data in cells A3 through B10. You determine the type of pie chart. Provide an appropriate title for the chart and appropriate percentage labels.
3. Insert a pie chart icon, found in the *Analytics* category.
4. Apply the Transparent, Colored Outline - Accent 4 graphic style (fifth column, last row) to the icon.
5. Position the pie chart icon in the lower right corner of the worksheet.
6. Print only the worksheet containing the chart.
7. Save and then close **U2-EPProdDept**.

Assessment 6

Use the PMT Function and Apply Formatting to a Workbook

1. Open **HERSalesInfo** and then save it with the name **U2-HERSalesInfo**.
2. The owner of Hilltop Equipment Rental is interested in selling three tractors owned by the business and needs to determine the possible monthly income from the sales. Using the PMT function, insert a formula in cell E4 that calculates monthly payments. (Type a minus symbol [–] before the cell designation in the *Pv* text box at the Function Arguments dialog box.)
3. Copy the formula in cell E4 into cells E5 and E6.
4. Insert a formula in cell F4 that multiplies the amount in cell E4 by the amount in cell D4.
5. Copy the formula in cell F4 into cells F5 and F6.
6. Insert a formula in cell G4 that subtracts the amount in cell B4 from the amount in cell F4. **Hint: The formula should return a positive number.**
7. Copy the formula in cell G4 into cells G5 and G6.
8. Save, print, and then close **U2-HERSalesInfo**.

Assessment 7

Use the IF Function and Apply Formatting to a Workbook

1. Open **PSQtrlySales** and then save it with the name **U2-PSQtrlySales**.
2. Insert an IF statement in cell F4 that inserts *Yes* if cell E4 contains a number greater than 74999 and inserts *No* if the number in cell E4 is not greater than 74999. Copy the formula in cell F4 to the range F5:F18. Center-align the text in the range F4:F18.
3. Insert a footer with your name at the left, the current date in the middle, and the current time at the right.
4. Turn on the display of formulas, print the worksheet in landscape orientation, and then turn off the display of formulas. (The worksheet will print on two pages.)
5. Save and then close **U2-PSQtrlySales**.

Assessment 8

Insert a Text Box and Hyperlinks in a Travel Workbook

1. Open **TravDest** and then save it with the name **U2-TravDest**.
2. Insert a text box in the workbook with the following specifications:
   a. Draw the text box at the right of the image.
   b. Type Call 1-888-555-1288 for last-minute vacation specials!
   c. Select the text and then change the font to 24-point Forte, change the fill to No fill, and apply the standard blue color.
   d. Size and position the text box so it appears visually balanced with the travel image.
3. Make sure you are connected to the internet and then for each city in the worksheet, search for sites that might be of interest to tourists. Write down the web address of the best web page you find for each city.
4. Create a hyperlink with each city name to the web address you wrote down in Step 3. (Select the hyperlink text in each cell and change the font size to 18 points.)
5. Test each hyperlink to make sure you entered the web address correctly. Click the hyperlink and then close the web browser after the page has displayed.
6. Save, print, and then close **U2-TravDest**.

Assessment 9

Insert an Image and a SmartArt Graphic in a Workbook

1. Open **SalesQuotas** and then save it with the name **U2-SalesQuotas**.
2. Insert a formula in cell C3 using an absolute reference to determine the projected quotas at a 10% increase of the current quotas.
3. Copy the formula in cell C3 to the range C4:C12. Apply the Accounting format with two digits after the decimal point and a dollar symbol [$] to cell C3.
4. In row 1, insert the **Money** image from your EL1U2 folder (or search online for an image related to money and then insert the image). You determine the size, position, and formatting of the image. If necessary, increase the height of the row.
5. Insert the Pyramid List SmartArt graphic at the right of the data. Insert the following quota ranges in the rectangle shapes and apply the specified fill colors. *Note: The bottom rectangle shape will contain the range $50,000 to $99,999.*

   $50,000 to $99,999 (apply a green color)
   $100,000 to $149,999 (apply a blue color)
   $150,000 to $200,000 (apply a red color)

6. Apply formatting to the SmartArt graphic to enhance the appearance.
7. Insert a custom header with your name at the left, the current date in the middle, and the file name at the right.
8. Change the orientation to landscape and make sure the SmartArt graphic fits on the page.
9. Save, print, and then close **U2-SalesQuotas**.

Assessment 10

Insert a Symbol, WordArt, and Screenshot in a Sales Workbook

1. Open **CISales** and then save it with the name **U2-CISales**.
2. Delete the text *Landower Company* in cell A7 and then type Económico in the cell. (Use the Symbol dialog box to insert *ó*.)
3. Insert a new row at the beginning of the worksheet.
4. Select and then merge cells A1 through D1.
5. Increase the height of row 1 to 141.00 points.
6. Insert the text *Custom Interiors* as WordArt in cell A1. You determine the formatting of the WordArt. Move and size the WordArt so it fits in cell A1.
7. Open Word and then open **CICustomers** from your EL1U2 folder. Click the Excel button and with **U2-CISales** open, make a screenshot (using the *Screen Clipping* option) of the customer information in the Word document. Position the screenshot image below the data in the cells.
8. Insert a custom footer with your name at the left and the file name at the right.
9. Make sure the data in the cells and the screenshot display on the same page and then print the worksheet.
10. Save and then close **U2-CISales**.
11. Make Word the active program, close **CICustomers**, and then close Word.

Assessment 11

Insert and Format a Shape in a Budget Workbook

1. Open **SEExpenses** and then save it with the name **U2-SEExpenses**.
2. Make the following changes to the worksheet so it displays as shown in Figure U2.1:
   a. Select and then merge cells A1 through D1.
   b. Add fill to the cells as shown in Figure U2.1. (Use the Green, Accent 6, Lighter 40% fill color in the last column, fourth row in the *Theme Colors* section.)
   c. Increase the height of row 1 to the approximate size shown in Figure U2.1.
   d. Make cell A1 active, type SOLAR, press Alt + Enter, and then type ENTERPRISES. Format the text you just typed in 20-point Calibri bold and change the font color to Green, Accent 6, Darker 25% (last column, fifth row in the *Theme Colors* section). Center and middle-align the text in the cell.
   e. Insert the sun shape (in the *Basic Shapes* section of the Shapes button drop-down list). Apply the Gold, Accent 4, Lighter 40% shape fill (eighth column, fourth row in the *Theme Colors* section) and change the shape outline to Green, Accent 6, Darker 25% (last column, fifth row). Copy the shape in the cell and then size and position the shapes as shown in the figure.
3. Save, print, and then close **U2-SEExpenses**.

Figure U2.1 Assessment 11

	A	B	C	D
1	SOLAR ENTERPRISES			
2	*Expense*	*Actual*	*Budget*	*% of Actual*
3	Salaries	$ 126,000.00	$ 124,000.00	98%
4	Benefits	25,345.00	28,000.00	110%
5	Commissions	58,000.00	54,500.00	94%
6	Media space	8,250.00	10,100.00	122%
7	Travel expenses	6,350.00	6,000.00	94%
8	Dealer display	4,140.00	4,500.00	109%
9	Payroll taxes	2,430.00	2,200.00	91%
10	Telephone	1,450.00	1,500.00	103%
11				

Writing Activities

The following activities give you the opportunity to practice your writing skills and demonstrate your understanding of some of the important Excel features you have mastered in this unit. Use correct grammar, appropriate word choices, and clear sentence constructions.

Activity

1

Prepare a Projected Budget

You are the accounting assistant in the Financial Department of McCormack Funds and you have been asked to prepare a proposed annual department budget. The total amount available to the department is $1,450,000. You are given these percentages for the proposed budget items: salaries, 45%; benefits, 12%; training, 14%; administrative costs, 10%; equipment, 11%; and supplies, 8%. Create a worksheet with this information that shows the projected yearly budget, the budget items in the department, the percentage for each item, and the amount for each item. After the worksheet is completed, save the workbook and name it **U2-MFBudget**. Print and then close the workbook.

Optional: Using Word, write a memo to members of the McCormack Funds Finance Department explaining that the proposed annual department budget is attached for their review. Comments and suggestions are to be sent to you within one week. Save the file and name it **U2-MFMemo**. Print and then close the file.

Activity	**Create a Travel Tours Bar Chart**
2	Prepare a worksheet in Excel for Carefree Travels that includes the following information:

Scandinavian Tours

Country	Tours Booked
Norway	52
Sweden	62
Finland	29
Denmark	38

Use the information in the worksheet to create and format a bar chart in a separate worksheet. Save the workbook and name it **U2-CTTours**. Print only the worksheet containing the chart and then close **U2-CTTours**.

Activity	**Prepare a Ski Vacation Worksheet**
3	Prepare a worksheet for Carefree Travels that advertises a snow skiing trip. Include the following information in the announcement:

- At the beginning of the worksheet, create a company logo that includes the company name *Carefree Travels* and an image related to travel.
- Include the heading *Whistler Ski Vacation Package* in the worksheet.
- Include the following details below the heading:
  - Round-trip air transportation: $395
  - Seven nights' hotel accommodations: $1,550
  - Four all-day ski passes: $425
  - Compact rental car with unlimited mileage: $250
  - Total price of the ski package: (calculate the total price)
- Include the following information somewhere in the worksheet:
  - Book your vacation today at special discount prices.
  - Two-for-one discount at many of the local ski resorts.

Save the workbook and name it **U2-CTSkiTrips**. Print and then close the workbook.

Internet Research

Find Information on Excel Books and Present the Data in a Worksheet

Locate two companies on the internet that sell new books. At the first new book company site, locate three books on Microsoft Excel. Record the title, author, and price for each book. At the second new book company site, locate the same three books and record the prices. Create an Excel worksheet that includes the following information:

- Name of each new book company
- Title and author of each book
- Prices for each book from the two book company sites

Create a hyperlink to the website of each book company. Then save the completed workbook and name it **U2-Books**. Print and then close the workbook.

Job Study

Create a Customized Time Card for a Landscaping Company

You are the manager of Landmark Landscaping Company and are responsible for employee time cards. At the New backstage area, search for and download a time card using the words *weekly time sheet portrait* to narrow the search. Use the template to create a customized time card workbook for your company. With the workbook based on the template open, insert additional blank rows to increase the spacing above the *Employee* row. Insert an image related to landscaping or gardening and position and size it attractively in the form. Include a text box with the text *Lawn and Landscaping Specialists* inside the box. Format, size, and position the text attractively in the form. Fill in the form for the current week with the following employee information:

   Employee: Jonathan Holder
   Manager: (Your name)
   Employee phone: (225) 555-3092
   Employee email: None
   Regular hours: 8 hours for Monday, Tuesday, Wednesday, and Thursday
   Overtime: 2 hours on Wednesday
   Sick hours: None
   Vacation: 8 hours on Friday
   Rate per hour: $20.00
   Overtime pay: $30.00

Save the completed form and name it **U2-TimeCard**. Print and then close **U2-TimeCard**.